THE ORACLE TRAVELS LIGHT

THE ORACLE TRAVELS LIGHT

PRINCIPLES OF MAGIC

W I T H   C A R D S

CAMELIA ELIAS

EYECORNER PRESS

THE ORACLE TRAVELS LIGHT:
PRINCIPLES OF MAGIC WITH CARDS

Published by EYECORNER PRESS
August 2015

ISBN: 978-87-92633-28-6

Cover design, photo composition, and layout:
Camelia Elias

Printed in the UK and US

CONTENTS

102, NO-SELF-
Le Pendue

§

§

Acknowledgements

I am grateful to all those who claim that I am not done with this kind of work, urging me to do more.

People who seek my advice in confidence. Thank you for your trust. Without your questions there would be no magic.

My family, who believes I can do things others can't: Bent, Manna, Søren, and Paul. You are all patient, kind, and generous. Thank you.

My friends, K. Frank Jensen and Witta Kiessling Jensen for opening their hearts and house of spirits to me. I bow to you.

Anthony Johnson, for the continuous flow of magic. Thank you for the alchemy of song and soul.

My peyote tribe, Apache Peyote chief, Hector Ibarra, and fire chief, Hesi Durbin. Thank you for allowing my cartomantic temple to enter yours.

Shaman Annette Høst. Thank you for your common sense and wisdom, and the beauty of the circle.

My students of cards and magic, particularly Elizabeth Owen and Josie Close. Thank you for allowing me to use chuncks of examples from your natural magic and spellcrafting cycles respectively.

I'm grateful for the fun in the fanfare of cards, always heralding new times beyond time. Thank you to all my divination mothers.

For K. Frank Jensen
and Witta Kiessling Jensen

magical friends and collectors of cards and spirits

MAGIC IN THE SPINE

Her charms can cure what souls she Please,
Rob other hearts of heartful ease,
Turn rivers backward to their source,
And make the stars forget their course,
And call up ghosts from night.

−The Aeneid, BK. IV. 487-491

In my work with the Tarot cards I always associate the art of reading the image with magic: the magic of storytelling. Well known writers have long agreed that a good story is a story that combines skill, seduction, and mythology. From novelist Italo Calvino, who was obsessed with the Tarot cards, to novelist Vladimir Nabokov, who was obsessed with butterflies, we have received the idea that the best art is the art of knowing how to use your storytelling elements in such a way that they make your hair rise on your back. You can only think so much; you can only permute with your ideas so much; you can only teach so much; if you don't write with your spine, your story is form and content minus magic.

In my work with the cards I'm attracted to how the element of enchantment is a given, a gift, rather than something I must work through or towards, as might be the case in a creative writing project. Whenever I lay down three cards, the first realization I make is, precisely, that nothing is made, but all is given. What do I mean by this in concrete terms?

Let me give an example of a recurrent question. Not so long ago a fan of my writings on my cartomantic website, *Taroflexions,* said something about how lovely it would be if I would 'spill the beans in a dumbed down manner so that us not so smart folk can pick up that wisdom about cards and magic.' I made the following remark, which also became a recipe for a magical experience. I reproduce my advice here, in a slightly altered form that fits this introduction. This is what I said:

'If magic wants something from you, it will tell you. Try this: take a pack of cards with you to a quiet place in nature. Go to a nice tree at dusk, after sunset. Sit by it. Tell it that you want to read the cards like a devil, or an angel, or a god. It's up to you, really. But be honest about it. Whoever you imagine you want to read the cards like, be honest about her name. State your purpose with an inflamed heart. Think of me, if you like. Then sit some more. Feel the warmth of the cards in your hands. How do your hands feel? Are they transparent yet? Can you swear that your fingers know all the cards by heart? Good. Ask your question. Be honest about it. Ask what you really want to know, not what you think you should ask. Don't be polite. Be violent in your question. The wind in the leaves can be gentle or brutal, so don't worry about overdoing it. You do want to read the cards like a god, don't you? Lay down three cards. Look at what's on them. Don't think. Not yet. Just look at the cards. You feel like stumbling. Remember you sit on top of old roots. They are not kidding about why they are there. Why should you? Look at the cards and let them formulate the logic of what you see. There will be logic,

logic of the most solid kind. You get your answer. Say thank you for the wisdom and leave an offering. Walnuts is a good idea. They look like a brain. You will want to use yours. You will be ready for it. Magic is no mystery. It's just there. It will take you places higher than you imagine – if it wants to. And if not, you will still have read the cards like a god. Can you ask for more? You cannot. Live magically. It's the only obligation. And then wait. The magic itself will revisit you. It will check on you. Show it your commitment. Do you even have a choice? Get real. What else is there? Conventions? Lord have mercy on our souls.

I'll say this: practice makes perfect. If you are missing something, it's listening. And don't worry about the incredulous, or all the writers who make claims to rationality and debunk magical thinking. They can talk, but they can't listen. Hence they miss out on a number of things. They are too impatient to get their point across. But what is that point? If you 'listen' to their writings, you will realize that it's filled with anxiety and fundamental fears. Such writing is devoid of the wisdom of real common sense. Why waste time on prose like that? Give yourself time. That's the only trick. There is no woo anywhere. It's just yourself disciplining yourself into doing something you will resist. Get your senses in there, all of them, and listen to your environment. Getting yourself in a most vigilant state and sharpening your acuity is the most difficult, but it can be done.

The only requirement is to listen. Really listen. You won't feel the need for the 'rational' folks to come and rescue you from your silliness. You will be there between the worlds praising your luck for being able to say to yourself: 'I'm alive and I know it.' This is the only kind of knowing that you need. Good luck.'

The above advice me think about how we *know* magic. I asked the cards. Three of them fell on the table: **The Hermit, The Devil, The Star.**

They suggested the following: First we seek it, and then we have a few encounters. We get to move between the below and the above. The Devil enthralls us, and the Star releases us.

Perhaps the idea is to become skilled enough at reading the signs, so that we may move between the planes of perception without worrying about a thing. When we decide to 'do' magic, we realize that 'doing' magic is receiving. We are thus in a state that already exceeds our expectations. Some would call it the beginning of surrendering. We do not enter the magical realm because we have expectations, but because we want to live fully. Living fully has little to do with 'what we make of it', with what we expect to 'see'. If we see anything, it is just this: the manifestation of things coming together and validating that what we are doing is the right thing.

Magic begins when we see that there's a direct alignment between our intentions and the manifestation of what prompts our intentions. Once we get to see this we can be sure that our magic is there, where 'there' is home, the familiar, and the recognition of the forces of nature as they give themselves to us in grace.

When we play cards, when we play with the cards, we find ourselves in the proximity of old wisdom; the wisdom that was brilliant enough to think of ways of stylizing the powers of nature. What are the four suits in a pack of cards? Nature, our own bodies, and prompters for action. The cups suggest our blood, and the way it circulates in our bodies. Without our blood streaming we're dead. With the diamonds or the coins we make transactions. We can feel our adrenaline making our blood hot when we're about to close a deal that's important to us. Having your brain on fire is no small thing. With the clubs or the batons we build dwellings or compete. They have the energy of the wind. Before they are cut down, tall trees know who whispers in their leaves. With spades or swords we dig the earth, we go to war to conquer territory, more land, more earth. Before the spades were made for war they were minerals, iron attracting our blood. It is for this reason that within the context of magical folk traditions the suit of spades is considered the suit of the craft, or witchcraft.

As many archeological discoveries show, the first magical awareness began in sacrifice. Blood magic is still popular today, and is considered by some to be the most efficient. Blood attracts spirit. As spirit seeks embodiment, what better invitation than to use your own blood? Christians have gone over to bread and wine for their magical workings, but some question the necessity of making such a replacement of flesh and blood with bread and wine. What's a symbol without a voice? But to each their own.

Personally I ask of my magic and my cards one thing only: Does it work? Do I get a sense of direction when I look at what story emerges against the background of a sequence of images? While making considerations for how my magic works, based on what is given to me that also makes my spine tingle, I have figured out the following: It is awfully important to not only know myself, but to also know my place. Knowing how to relate what I know about myself to the place I inhabit is a wonderful exercise in being aware of how I act in the world. What motivates me? Why am I doing what I'm doing? To what extent can I determine that whatever I'm doing, I'm doing for the right reason, and not because I need others to give me stuff, such as stability, honors, reputation, a family, and so on? Can I know myself in all of these cultural constraints? Do I actually want to be where I am right now? Magic is about serving. But in order to serve others well, you must make the effort to learn what they need without prejudice. That's the hard part, and therefore the most magical.

Asking these questions requires some brutal honesty, and the answer may not always be pleasant, as it may lead to some drastic actions. But guess what, if we can see past the regular clichés – 'this is how we should or ought to think today, because Santa Claus has just dictated it' – we will realize that there's more to ourselves than we can imagine. There's more to ourselves than other people's diagnosis or perception of us, for better or worse.

Magic begins to happen when we start asking ourselves the nasty questions, the disturbing questions. There's no mystery to magic. There's just us having the courage of confrontation: 'Me, in the mirror.' Change doesn't start with what others tell us is efficient. Change starts with our getting humble. Kissing the ground we stand on, and acknowledging that we stand on a pile of bones. Ashes to ashes. We can all draw on this ancestral power. See what it feels like to consider the telluric forces of the earth as having to do with all the dead and buried that have come before us. Nothing is more efficient than realizing that we love ourselves with the highest power there is, our own breath, and that we do it for the right reason.

When I wish people to live magically, I realize instantly that we already do, or that they do too. They just don't know it yet. Often too much culture comes in our way. We are too concerned with 'image', our image, but we forget that this concern never reflects 'our' image, but always that of another. No wonder so many walk about thinking that they're missing something. But things are really simple. The magical life starts with forgetting a few cultural things. As soon as that happens, we're there, where 'there' simply means the space that allows us to see ourselves in alternative contexts to the ones provided by the cultures we live in. And then act accordingly.

Working with the cards enhances this very understanding of what we can be, independently of dictations. Our culture at large will not endorse such working with the cards, or some other tools that make us reflect on our human condition, as such work doesn't serve its general interests. Culture has a way of suggesting that what we're doing is never good enough, that what we are is never good enough. The more guilt culture instills in us, the more it stands to earn for itself. If we can't manage, there's Prozac at the pharmacy, or a consecrated shrink who can help us with our feeling of being disconnected. The more culture wins, the more we keep losing.

In my work with the cards, I experience one of the highest magical acts the moment when people realize that they can, in fact, tell themselves the following: 'Now I'll pay attention to everything for my own sake, rather than for the sake of what's expected of me.' But we all need to make that decision consciously. Yet this conscious decision to say it out loud requires boldness and honesty. This doesn't always appeal to everyone consulting the cards, tacitly allowing the cards to work magic in their lives, but if they want to get there fast, rather than, say, after 30 years in therapy, then there's no other way.

The interplay between cards and magic is found in the desire to push forward and beyond having to say: 'Wow, this exceeds what I'm thinking, what I've been expecting.' What we want is not to *think,* but to *live* magic in action. Thinking will be integrated into that action, so it becomes redundant in the larger scheme. In principle, all that is man-made must go. It must simply fall down, like the Tower in the Tarot.

Where magical awareness is concerned, we must realize that all that we have learnt and built for ourselves in the image of some cultural pre-conditioning must be smashed. We do not approach magic from any tower, whether of wisdom, constraint, or any other such constructions.

Magic may be the thing of our hands and thoughts, and our capacity to discern, but it is also raw power. It is this raw power that we want to re-discover and use.

The cards can help us.

The purpose of this book is to say something about the ways in which cards and magic are always interrelated. They are not separate. In my examples of reading the cards for various questions, what I'm interested in is precisely the conflation of tool with totem, where totem indicates a symbolic awareness of the physical manifestation of metaphysical desires, be that desires for change, or for learning, or for bending others' will in alignment with what we want to achieve for ourselves and others.

Yet unlike in my other cartomantic book, *Marseille Tarot: Towards the Art of Reading* (2015), where I have introduced the readers to a method of reading the cards, in this book I'm interested in exploring how our guiding skills, the ability to enchant and to raise magical awareness, can be successfully employed in the work of transforming our place. With the transformation of our place, with the ability to make it a magical place, by sanctifying it with our presence, we enhance our understanding of ourselves in context. As our selves are relational selves, the best way to go about our process of self-understanding is to start with exploring our geographies, both the mental and the physical.

A few of the ideas presented here have been explored on *Taroflexions,* but the way they come together in this book – to serve the unified notion of how we may best serve our community in terms of practicing our interpretative arts skillfully and magically – will be a novel approach.

Strap yourselves with a cordon of cards.

We're going for a new ride.

TERMS, POSITION, AND STRUCTURE

MAGIC: I refer to this term as it relates to both the experience of marvel in general, and the experience of influencing events to produce marvel.

MAGICIAN: Someone who participates in producing marvels using hidden, natural forces. The magician can effect change that is both tangible and intangible. The magician using cards as a tool for her magic can do both, divine and seek advice, and intervene and change the course of a situation. With specific cards the magician can create a physical talisman for protection or some other need, devise a herbal bath for purification, make an invocation, or cast binding spells. The magician can also effect change that is intangible to the extent that she can use her skills to fix someone's blind spot. The actual, physical effect of suggesting spiritual or metaphysical solutions for improving someone's situation takes place when the person seeking advice or intervention directly acts upon it. Here's an example:

> **Client:** 'I can't get pregnant.'
> **The cards say:** 'Establish a relation of equality in your household first, and then it will happen.'
> **Client:** 'Well, it's true that my partner is not quite ready yet.'
> **The card reader:** 'Then get yourself on the same page on this issue, and then it will happen.'

The line between advice and intervention is not a thick one, as it relies on the power of suggestion to effect concrete change. Magic occurs at the intersection of the mentally based intention, with the indirect suggestion that activates the unconscious, and finally, with the physical grounding of both intention and suggestion in concrete action. Or else, magic happens at the intersection of mind and body in symbolic acts that follow a specifically formulated intention to effect change.

Mental magic without some concrete 'doing' – be that in the form of a ritual, scribbling sigils on parchment, or invoking elemental or planetary powers – remains in the realm of wishful thinking and the imagination, so here I clearly distinguish between acts of visualization and the necessity to ground them in the material plane of action.

Skillful magicians do not always need a whole arsenal of props and costumes to effect a mental construct for intervention. In other words, in practical magic we may not always have to advise the practitioner to make sure to have her broom handy whenever she needs to fly over to the otherworld. A snapping of the fingers can also do. By grounding one's visual and mental images in the physical plane, I mean any act of using prompters or a token that have been invested with the magician's breath, gaze, or gesture for the purpose of performing a magical act.

Finally, the term 'Magician' covers the following related functions: sorcerer, witch, shaman, fortuneteller.

OTHERWORLD: This term designates the space that exceeds our ordinary perception. It is the place we consciously go to when we want to try something else than the regular cultural pre-conditioning we are all subject to. Some call this space, the imagination, fantasy, fairytale, madness. I like the definition of the otherworld that scholar Susan Greenwood gives in her book, *Magic, Witchcraft and the Otherworld* (2000): 'The otherworld is a secret world with flexible boundaries' (25).

In shamanic parlance, which I also draw on, the otherworld is another aspect, or dimension of our ordinary reality in this world.

The otherworld is experienced through a magician's skills regarding moving energy consciously.

To the extent that the magician operates with shifts in consciousness, she allows herself to cross thresholds into worlds that are not subject to cultural hierarchies and dictations. In this sense, it should not come as a surprise that once the magician has left behind worrying about her social image, or about what the neighbor might have to say about her nocturnal activities, she can encounter a greater power than the one ruling over her mundane life, ensuring that everything has a purpose according to the dominant normative codes.

For the magician, the otherworld is the world where she can breathe the air of freedom and work with power as spirit that teaches her about her place in the world. Man is not the center of all things, hence, paying attention to the animal and plant kingdoms, the movement of stars, and the dead we live with, is the first lesson to learn. Consequently, the otherworld is a source of knowledge that exceeds the cultural consecrations of our ordinary world and reality. Among other things, the function of this knowledge is to raise the magician above superstition to the level where she becomes an adept precisely at paying attention. Once you're able to see what's what, chances are that you will also be able to distinguish between what's essential and what's not in relation to what you need to perform.

POSITION

The above brings me to my own position in relation to my understanding and practice of magic. For instance, the only difference between scholarly knowledge and magical knowledge is that the first is institutionalized whereas the latter is not. Culturally speaking, the one who works for the prediction market on Wall Street has a better reputation than the one who does the same at every fortunetelling parlor in New York; the psychoanalyst has a better reputation than the spiritual teacher who organizes shamanic weekend classes. And so it goes.

In this book I adopt the position of the scholar *cum* magical practitioner, which is to say that, while I'm interested in developing a clearly descriptive and reflective level of what I'm trying to achieve here, I also bring to my writing the experiential level of magic as derived from my ability to read visual texts, decode a message from the cards by following a method, and understand and evaluate what is at stake in the context of a question or search for solutions to a particular problem. My magical ability to distinguish between contexts, narratives, and different worlds I may happen to move within is no different than my academic ability to do the same, whenever I approach the task of researching a topic in order to find a solution to a problem, or offer a novel worldview about it.

I see no difference in my work with the cards between the way in which I read the cards for a university professor of mathematics, who struggles with how he can formalize a proof for his theorem, and the way I do the same for the single mother who is at war with her former partner. I see my magic as a way of living the life of the stories we create. The more interesting, sophisticated, exciting, and full of life force these stories are, the better I can perform being the in world; the better I can evaluate the value of my own presence in the world. Magic is not something I believe in. In fact, I have repeatedly stated elsewhere that I'm a Marxist with a penchant for the oracular, the voice in poetry that allows us to articulate the truth, and the philosophy of action that entices us to embody states that are beneficial to ourselves and others beyond the trendy and the trivial.

Magic for me is simply seeing more and acting better.

STRUCTURE

The first six chapters in this book tackle the idea of storytelling, enchantment, and magic with cards. Through personal stories, I reflect on how we can define a magical prompt, what we understand by the law of similitude and correspondence, how we can invoke the dead, and what we make of magic and morality.

In my examples I read the cards with view to making extrapolations as to how we walk a particular magical path, and how we know it's the right one for us.

I also go behind the situation of reading the cards, and look at the difference between our cognitive faculty that enables us to decode and interpret a visual message and our psychological responses that may be the result of transference and the recognition of familiar cultural patterns. Here I'm interested in where we can locate the truth so that the reading of the cards stands in sharp contrast to processes of self-delusion and wishful thinking.

The last two chapters consist of practical magic. One chapter is dedicated to four rituals based on natural magic, as derived from reading the cards. The other is an introduction to spellcrafting and an original method of how to go about it.

What I bring to the community of magicians and diviners that's new is my commitment to demonstrating how we can devise with cards the most efficient rituals for practical magic, rather than having to go to sources unfamiliar to us and our cultural background, which are often beyond our grasp.

MAGICAL PROMPT: 'I KNEW IT'

Great stories happen to those who can tell them.

– Old adage

In my writings and teachings about cards I emphasize not only the power of storytelling, but also the power of suggestion[1]. Usually this latter power functions as a bridge that links what we see in the cards with the magic of recognizing what we need to do beyond verbal expression. The sense of inhabiting a magical space while looking at the cards becomes quite prominent when we realize that what we find beyond the words that the cards have just enabled us to articulate is a strong sense of how our bodies respond to a situation.

So when we lay down three cards and the story of our situation starts unfolding, we begin to perceive how our heads shift position with our hearts. We may look at ourselves and experience the magic of having our thoughts, or cognitive capacity for decoding messages, travel to our hearts, or, conversely, we may find our hearts, or emotional charge in your cognitive perception travel to the seat of our rational selves, often the head.

---

1 Some parts of this section have been published in *The Cartomancer: A Quarterly Tarot, Lenormand & Oracle Journal*. Vol. 1, Issue 1. Summer 2015. Portland, Oregon: Devera Publishing.

The magic begins when we find that, although we may express one thing in our question, perhaps as dictated by our rational capacity to reflect on what we need to ask about, the cards may indicate something else, picturing wearing our emotions on our sleeves, our thoughts in the gut, and our hearts instead of our heads rationalizing our emotions.

The magic begins when we are forced to address our own reluctance to disclose verbally what we 'really' want to know. Any cartomancer will have come across this situation a countless number of times. Culturally speaking, it is also precisely this situation that makes us understand why work with the cards has been demonized, ridiculed, or dismissed, as any dominant system interested in dictations would not put up with the sudden personal insights that people seeking advice from the cards can get, which, more often than not, would run counter to the very ideology that any dominant system wants to promote.

For example, the cards may indicate that instead of being anguished about loving two people at the same time, having to choose between them, one may as well go with the temptation to cross whatever the mainstream culture has deemed as appropriate. Will the mainstream culture approve of such deviant behavior? Of course not. How will this culture, then, represent the fortuneteller? As a Devil in disguise. What about the person going to the fortuneteller? A self-deluded poor sod.

In and of itself, stereotypical representations of anything that can help us understand ourselves a little better are bound to give us all a one-sided story of what is really going on, namely, our trying to carve for ourselves a space that is not merely informed by random dictations. Consequently, what interests me here is the other half of the story; the story of how we can act more truthfully and forcefully out of a place we can claim is finally ours. How is this story construed and in whose image? Does this story leave some space for others to inhabit? How does this space look, as it is infused already by our own presence? A presence, however, that is hopefully more interesting than the presence that ghosts other rooms and other voices.

LISTENTING TO THE CUE

A good story begins in the very moment when we allow ourselves to be prompted by the ways in which the cards invite us to address the split between our rational and sensual selves, or the gap between our heads and our hearts. Once we get a cue, we can think of it as a prompter for the next line. From there, all we need is power of observation and discernment. Not everything is essential and not everything addresses the context of the question. We have our question, and the cards will have an answer. Always.

But where do we begin, and how do we make sure that we don't drown in cues, or in seeing signs all over the place? How do we distinguish between the essential and the inessential? When I read the cards I start out of a premise that although I expect the cards to give me a relevant message that pertains to my concern, I actually try to think of the message in terms of information. Why is this so? Logically speaking, there's no message that we can deem useful that is not already part of a thinking process.

To begin with, what we receive from the cards is information, not messages. What turns this information into useful knowledge, which we then can think of in terms of a message, is process. As some good epistemologists have argued, there's no knowledge without the processing of information. What others call an intuitive reading is still a way of processing the information. As processing involves both mental work and our involved emotions, I think of the act of reading cards as an act of recognizing an emerging pattern against the background of how we define ourselves in context, as cultural selves and as selves in search of escaping cultural pre-conditioning.

Let me give an example of just what kind of mental and emotional work I engage in, when I look at a string of cards. For a snappy reading that reinvigorates my capacity to pay attention, my favorite is the 3-card sequence with the trumps. For clarifying information I use 2 cards from the deck that includes the pip cards and the court cards.

Let us also look at a classical question about love. A woman wanted to know where she and her lover were standing in relation to one another. The context for this question was a separation.

Three cards fell on the table:

The Wheel of Fortune, The Tower, The World

First off, if we go with assessing the cards based on what we've learnt from most contemporary books on the tarot, which describe each card in terms of the aim to learn a lesson and thus elevate ourselves above our condition, we could say that the World in the final position may indicate a chance for reconciliation. The World is, after all, a card that emphasizes accomplishment. But what if this accomplishment functions here as a full stop to this relationship?

Judging by the figure of the woman in the middle of her world, standing there on one foot all by herself, we could say that this card is representative of the situation when we cannot talk about 'us'. There is no 'us' here. There's only one woman doing her thing – whatever that is.

I suggested this much to the woman I was reading the cards for. But then I noticed an insistence in her body language for a firmer confirmation: 'Really, are 'we' really over?'

I grabbed the rest of my deck. Armed with a handful of pip and court cards, I repeated the initial question, but then I added a tag to it, which I formed according to the woman's facial expression and sense of excitement. After all, her heart was about to sink. She was right there at the crossroad of her ambiguity and ambivalence.

I asked again on her behalf: 'Is the World card a card that leads to elevation, to everything that this woman has ever wished for?' Or does it simply mean: 'That's it. You've come full circle on this one?' With this I mind, I have also recalled the initial question: 'Where do we stand now?'

Two cards fell on the table, and the woman's heart dropped even more:

Two Batons, 4 Swords

I said: 'We go from a helping hand to a helping hand with the coffin. *Pax Vobiscum.'*

Now the woman's heart was on the floor.

'But why, then, why on earth, do I still do this? Why do I still hope, and what exactly am I hoping for?'

The woman's tone was desperate, and for a very good reason. The situation was three monkeys and a squeezed lemon(de) (from the Wheel, *La Roue,* to the World, *Le Monde*).

We were both holding our breath. How much longer can we stay mute, mourning the situation? The pack of cards has many more secrets in it. 'Can we get another cue?', the woman asked, looking avidly at the remaining cards in the pack.

Two more cards fell on the table:

Knight of Coins, Ace of Batons

At this point the woman went blank. She stared at the coin, then at the green, voluptuous twig. There was a connection. She knew it. But what was it?

At this point I entered the picture assuming full authority. I delivered a series of one-line statements in a detached way, and then she took over in direct dialogue with the cards and me. By this last draw, she was ready to read her own cards. Before I got to finish my sentence, she took over, and said:

'You're still hoping because there's the promise of money to be invested in strong life force. In goes a coin, and out pops ...'

'Sex? You mean, all I'm interested in is sex?'

'You said it,' I said.

Now, what had just happened there? Nothing happened but processing two levels of signification. One cultural and the other visual.

Let's take culture first:

The image of the Knight coming riding, and reflecting himself in the big coin, transmitted subliminally to the woman querent the suggestion that he actually has that coin. The implication of this is the following: The woman is likely to fall for that recognition – of associating the coin with comfort – because she is culturally prone to it. Why? Look at our history. We have a long line of examples when this equation, 'Man equals power, and power equals comfort' is true, for women, that is.

So when the woman asked: 'Why am I hoping,' when she could see how hopeless the love was, what with a broken tower in the middle of the sequence, then it's because she took a step down from her ideals. She regressed from the high, abstract concept of love to the material. She was ready to see the coin as the substitution for love.

Mirror, mirror on the wall, give me something to mourn over...

The assumption that we could then make here is that, ultimately, it was not love that this woman hoped for, but through the coin, she hoped that her desire for love would not stop. The meaning of this message was thus based on transference, and the exchange was the following: A coin for life. The golden coin transferred its light to the fresh, green twig. There was here the strong suggestion that if she stopped loving, she stopped living. Consequently, the woman still wanted this man, but not because she loved him. Rather, she wanted him because he was her ticket to staying alive. It's the 'story' of him that kept her alive.

Now let us look at the visual signification:

If we take the visual cues into consideration, we clearly get closer to having an explanation for the hopeless love and why the woman put sex on the table. Her rhetorical question to me, 'you mean, all I'm interested in is sex?' indicated a shift in her focus from the gender of the Knight to the shape of his coin, which she then placed in relation to the Ace. Understanding the cards the visual way makes us think of analogical connections: Round thing versus an erect thing. Does it ring any bells?

Now we can get back to the initial question again, and speculate on when the World card could be interpreted more positively. When it could give us license to say: 'Perfect. After a terrible bump, you'll get everything. You're standing at the door of the world, right on the threshold. Just enter'.

We would be able to say this only if the woman we're talking to is still involved with her man in some form or another. But, if she comes to the cartomancer with her question from the perspective of someone who is merely speculating about a long lost relationship, then we would have to go ahead and make her realize that the woman in the World card is alone, and that her 'standing' is quite literally on one foot. The two figures in the preceding card are dead. *Pax Vobiscum.*

The point here is that it makes sense to always insist on drawing not only on a very precisely formulated question, but also on its context, as the context makes it easier for us to determine just how much ambiguity we can handle. Anything else can just as well amount to an exercise in futility and waste of time, with pulling more cards from the deck until we finish it in the hope of getting the 'better message'.

When in doubt about the function of the trumps, certainly, we can pull some number cards, and then pull some more, and then finish the whole deck, but for that we'd need to decide that what we are after is to construe a narrative that proceeds from the cards, rather than from the question. The truth is that we can always tell a fascinating, endless story, but is this narrative going to answer the querent's question in a precise manner?

TRANSFERENCE

By using this example above I'm trying to demonstrate how by processing the information from the images on the cards, so that it becomes useful knowledge, we also engage in two other processes of transference.

First, we go from the cards to the querent. If successful, this transference often manifests as a simple conclusion: 'I see it, and I understand.' On the one hand, this affirmation is based on the activation of the conscious process of understanding (as our cultural pre-conditioning reflects how we define our needs in terms of other people's needs, or what other people want from us). On the other hand, this affirmation is also based on the activation of the unconscious process of realization (related to individual desire and the acknowledgment of personal need).

Second, we go from the reader to the querent. In this case, we must ask ourselves: What do we emphasize in a reading? In questions about love that has ended, do we focus on the qualities in the cards that disclose the reason why the querent hates the other, and why she should accept that they are over, or do we suggest ways in which she can get on with the program? What if the cards don't make any such suggestion? This happens all the time.

I will leave the reader to ponder on this open question, while suggesting the following: Before we consider where the cards come from, their history or esoterically imposed meanings, we may want to actually just read the cards. Make peace with the cards, say *Pax Vobiscum* to ourselves, nod silently, and acknowledge the story of, 'I knew it'.

Real magic happens when we experience a special kind of closeness to the personal story of the others. When we come closer and closer to their predicament, we get to see the world through their eyes. In this sense, the cards act as prompters for remembrance. The remembrance of our own lost loves.

Magic happens when we get to recuperate in this very loss something that is more valuable than love, which is life itself. Ultimately, we read cards for the story of ourselves, and not only for the story of others. But as we end up serving the community in ways that are less consecrated by culture at large, we discover the magic in us. The magic that strips us to the bare bones. And this has got to be the greatest gift of enchantment.

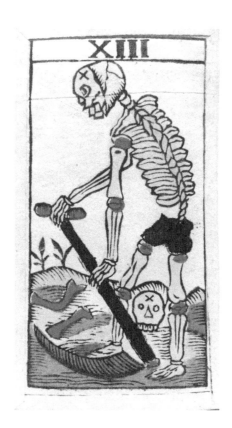

BRINGING DOWN THE BOWL

In fairy tales and playing cards, in myths and legends and rumors, in strange poems and old songs, we hid the secret knowledge.

— John Whiteside Parsons,
Freedom is a Two-Edged Sword

Magic for me is an appreciation of a specific mood that is either induced by ritual or ceremony, or that arises by itself when prompted through the activation of a heightened awareness about a certain event. This latter situation can manifest in very simple terms. Yet, as with all things magical, it proves nothing. What it does, however, and this is what I value the most, is take care of my experience of being astonished on a daily basis. And I have to admit that I'm addicted to being astonished. Everyday I look for something that will astonish me. Perhaps that's why I work with poetry, both in terms of producing it and in terms of studying it in the scholarly fashion.

As far as working with the cards, I can say that the images on the cards acquire magical status every time I think of them as prompters for processing my feelings in ways that enhance my cognitive capacity for decoding a message or an omen, for evaluating what I'm seeing or experiencing, and for understanding that we can easily take our cue for a better life from the direction that the cards point us towards.

But let me give a few concrete examples of what magic is to me, before I advance an argument as to what is at stake when we use cards in a magical context, and what the pay off is when we allow the cards to transform our worldview.

JACK OF TRADES

Since the famous occultist and rocket scientist Jack Parsons reminds me of my father who died in 1976, I tend to think of him on his birthday and of what it is that he shares with my father. They were both rocket scientists – my father worked for the military in Ineu, Romania, where they built missiles, Parsons for Caltech, in the Jet Propulsion Lab – they both died in their 30s, and they were both magicians.

On October 2 two years ago, I took my dog out for a walk, and while thinking of the two in tandem, two crows started following me on the road. I greeted them properly, as I decided that they were the two I'd been thinking of, the two Jacks – incidentally my father's nickname was also Jack (in Romanian, Gick). The crows said something, and I said something, and it was all very good. On the way back, I was intent on honoring them with cooking lunch for myself in the form of scrambled eggs and bone marrow (my father's favorite). I was very excited about this project, and I could see that the crows were too, judging by their circling and swirling around me. They followed me almost to the entrance to my block. I went upstairs, opened the fridge, and... the horror. There were no eggs in the fridge. What to do?

I couldn't let the two down, so I went out again and hit the local supermarket. I got two dozen eggs. That's 24 eggs in two egg cartons. I opened the first one and I gaped: 10 eggs were brown and 2 white. 'No way,' I said. At this point I was beginning to get a very clear sense of why I bought the second egg carton when I didn't need it. For proof. For you see, what would give me better proof of the two rocket-scientists having turned into crows than seeing that they have now have also turned into eggs? I figured that if the second egg carton would feature all the eggs brown, then that would be my proof. You can imagine my excitement. I opened the carton, and voilà: all the eggs were brown. So, out of 24 eggs bought on Jack Parsons's birthday, when I asked him specifically to hang out with my father and have a chat with him, two eggs turned out white. Does magic exist? Obviously it does. Incidentally, Jack Parsons's full name was John Whiteside Parsons (born Marvel Whiteside Parsons). White side marvel indeed. On that day, he was my man.

THE BOWL

Now, let me give another example.

Some 5 years ago, after a conference in Roskilde where I live, I invited some friends from the US over to dinner. We've known each other for ages, and we always meet regularly at an American Studies conference in Helsinki every other year. On this occasion the couple came over to my place, and I tried to explain to them something about my *Jugendstil* old clock on the wall, which to me resonates like the biggest cathedral in Denmark. After listening to its bong they concurred that it is very special.

When dinner was over and getting ready to leave, the woman told me by the door that she wanted to send me a gift from the US once she was back. She didn't say what it was.

Two years passed. I got nothing from the woman, and I didn't think too much of it. People are busy all the time. Then one day I fond myself in an occult shop in Oslo, trying out many Tibetan bowls on display. I didn't buy any, as these things come at an exorbitant price in Norway. But I was intent on going home and online immediately, in order to get some on ebay or some other such place.

Back in Roskilde I ended up spending the whole night, at least until 4 am, searching for Tibetan bowls and listening to various sound samples from around the globe. I had decided to buy three. Sensing my excitement and seeing me ready with my finger on my keyboard, pressing the 'buy it now' button, my partner asked me quickly: 'Where do those bowls ship from?' I said: 'The US.' 'Bad idea,' he said, 'you're going to pay customs and the price will amount to the same as you would have paid for them in Oslo.' Then he said: 'Wait until the morning, and we can both zip into town and visit a new age place.' I listened to him reluctantly. My finger was still burning with the desire to hit the button.

We finally went to bed. My finger had not cooled off yet. Eight o'clock in the morning the postman rang on the door. I was very sleepy as I only had 4 hours in bed. I went to the door moaning. I didn't expect any packages. I was trying to remember what books I had just ordered from Amazon. A bad habit. I opened the door and sure enough, a package. My partner asked me from the bedroom, also in an irritated tone, 'Who's it from?' I was astonished: 'Christ almighty,' I yelled, 'Tina sent her package. After two years!' I then muttered something along these lines, 'how nice that she remembered,' while unwrapping the gift. 'What's in it?,' the man wanted to know. I read the label: 'Bowl' it said, and then I shouted out more convincingly: 'It's a bowl' – while thinking, 'ceramics.' Then he said, being more perceptive or awake: 'Please don't tell me it's a Tibetan bowl.' 'No way,' I was thinking. I opened the box, and voilà, a Tibetan bowl. My partner fainted on the way to the bathroom. Absolutely perfect. Does magic exist? It goes to show. Does it have a name? No, it doesn't. It's a sinking into heavens.

My friend, Tina Parke-Sutherland, a lover of texts and sounds, saw my love of vibrations, but then she just had to wait two years to send her gift exactly at the right moment. When I pointed my finger at it. Adamantly. And that's all there is to it. Now I'm still bemused, saying to myself, 'how nice that I didn't have to go anywhere.' The Tibetan bowl was delivered on my doorstep when I wished for it the most.

THE BELL

Now, almost in the same vein as above, let me give you a final example, though not the last in my repertoire of magical happenings.

A week later after the above incident, I was organizing a conference at my home university. The participants were flying in from all the corners of the world. Some arrived a few days earlier. I invited a couple of friends into town to have dinner before the event proper. Over food and drinks, my partner, who was also the co-organizer, expressed concern with the coffee breaks that always drag too long, and the impossibility to get people back to the lecture rooms on time for the next panels. I said to him, 'you need a bell'. After dinner, we were strolling in the streets, and we passed a Tibetan place with lots of bells on display in the window. I said, 'oh, let's just enter and get you a bell, so you can gather the sheep.' 'No,' he said, 'I don't want to waste these people's time with your bells and kooky projects.' 'Ok,' I said. 'It's your hassle.' The next morning, the first to arrive at the conference was a woman from Japan. She gave us a present: A bell. Whoa, astonishment again. What magic! Needless to say, the bell was used throughout the entire conference to great effect. My partner didn't have to turn into a Lutheran fascist, disciplining everyone the insulting way, and I think he also thought better of my idea of bells and other kooky projects.

DOES MAGIC EXIST?

Now, as I started out saying, do these stories prove anything? The existence of magic, God, or some other such things that the incredulous are not so sure about? They prove nothing. But what they do is tell us what we can make of the way in which we interact with the world. By letting ourselves be enchanted with how things come to us, or with what happens when we point our index finger at someone or something, we get a sense of what it means to be alive beyond the blood pulsing through our veins. I like to think of old bones, dead people, and their breaths populating the atmosphere.

If I believe in anything I believe in this fact: The fact that we all live on top of one big cemetery. For all we know, those we bury don't go anywhere. They share their last breaths with all of us. There's gravity here. Even if ashes are spread, they still fall somewhere on the ground. Everything dies and everything gets recirculated. I believe in the magic of the bells ringing. For the dead and for myself. Perhaps it's this sound that makes our wishes find embodiment. When I ended up cooking Parsons and my Father with a splash of bone-marrow on my frying-pan, I sure had a good day. A totally magical day. Now, if a crow approaches me, I happen to ask it: which Jack are you? It usually answers. In this sense, I value the experience of magic above proof and rationality.

On a more mundane level, let's just say that the stories about the clock bonging, the bell ringing, and the bowl singing, offer me the following moral story: I never have to enter a Tibetan place. All I need to do is wish for something from there, and I get it instantly. I like that.

So magic for me is a mood enhancer. It is beyond proof and beyond dismissal. Magic, if we go with it, empowers us, and makes us think that if we can think it we can have it, even when we don't get it. I have hundreds of magical stories to tell, and so does everyone else who is interested in being astonished. That's all it takes. I simply tune in to what else is there beyond the measuring of how far our mental elastic stretches. As for rationality, I leave that to those who don't have anything better do to than to sit around and call others crazy.

In my work with the cards for magical purposes – which is to say that I use the cards both as prompters for bringing my awareness to the possibility of a derailed reality and as a bridge to analogical stories – I consider magic as a necessary condition for seeing what is happening in the cards the way a child would see. According to the dictionary of etymology, which gives us the history of how words have developed, magic is 'the art of influencing events and producing marvels using hidden natural forces.' We know that the cards are stylized versions of natural forces –

our blood in a cup, our forests in a stick, our earth under the spade, and our transactions in a coin – but the way in which all these forces come together for the magician to influence events and produce marvels is contingent on the kind of innocence that is devoid of hidden personal agendas. The magician who can make her conscious will part of her unconscious is a good magician, for that is where the art is; namely, in bringing together neutrality and passion, disinterest and devotion. When we can approach the cards like children, we get to learn what we can do with our magical intent – for better or worse.

A good magician also knows how to tap into the lost innocence of children. I still read fairytales. I grew up with some grusome ones from Russia and Germany. Then there were all the stories about the Dacian god, Zamolxis, and the power seat at Sarmizegetusa Regia in Romania, prior to the Romans conquering the Geto-Dacians in about AD 102. When to go to Romania I still visit the ruins, the timber circle resembling Stonehenge, and the Andesite Sun, a sundial witnessing the Dacians' connection to Hellenistic Greece, and their knowledge of astronomy and geometry.

As for my crossing of thresholds, if I don't snap my fingers to get there faster, I use a bell or a Tibetan bowl, my strong sense of smell, and a powerful plant given to me in a dream, the story of which you can hear about next.

TAKE THE WORMWOOD AND LEAVE THE UFO

My father died when I was eight. He is not someone I think of a lot, as I have very few memories of him. But some years ago I had a very powerful dream of him, which I immediately identified as a soul dream, or a dream that has shamanic proportions, as it teaches you something prophetic in a very elaborate, clear, and specific way.

I dreamt that I was standing on top of a sand dune on the West coast of Denmark, where I have a summerhouse.

As I was contemplating the tall grass, and smelling it too – smell being one of my main prompters for a shift in consciousness, whether I'm dreaming or awake – an UFO like airplane piloted by two men was making the rounds. I was amazed. It looked like a round capsule that behaved like an F-16 fighter jet when it puts up a military show. I instantly thought that I wanted to buy it. I went down from the top of the dune to a nearby place that now looked like a decrepit building in East Berlin. Inside the main room was an old woman dressed in a blue smock, sitting at a table. There was nothing else in the room. She looked like a factory worker, or a janitor, but it turned out that she was a healer. Behind me were a number of people waiting to go inside as well, and get a remedy for cuts, burns, injuries, small infections, and other such ailments.

I asked her about the price of the UFO, yet when she told me I sighed with regret, and said, 'I'm afraid I don't have that kind of money.' Then she said in Danish: 'You don't need that flying thing. You can use wormwood that is harvested in Sweden'. She then directed my gaze to what now was a whole mountain of wormwood in the very room we were in. She also said that I could travel by smoke, and then got really enthusiastic about telling me what she called 'marvelous stories about wormwood.' I didn't stay to listen, as I noticed that the line of people forming behind me got longer and longer, and I felt that I needed to give others a chance to talk to the woman.

Thus I got out of her place, and then I saw a house at a crossroad that looked just like an old Tirolese log house. My father was in the attic, and it seemed as if he was waiting for me. When he saw me he rushed out and came to embrace me. It was incredible. I have never had dreams of my dead father before this one. When he hugged me a smell like I'd never experienced before overwhelmed me. It was his smell. He was wearing a black leather jacket. After the kissing we then entered the house and went up to the room in the attic. There was only a table and one chair there. This room was very similar to the wormwood room, the only difference being that the walls here were made of wood, rather than concrete, hence the atmosphere was not sterile but warm.

My father put off his jacket, and he started rolling cigarettes. His hands were those of a sailor. He looked tough, and hardworking. I then noticed his elaborate tattoos – I don't remember my father having any tattoos, but when I told my sister about this dream, she assured me he had one. In my dream he looked like a pirate. After rolling his cigarettes at a slow pace, the first thing he said to me was this: 'You know, there are battles between the angels.' He used that word, 'angels', and that threw me aback for a moment, as I thought that only demons were into fighting.

Then he told me a lot about my sister, and what he thought she should do, and whom she should hang out with. He let me understand that he was not among the higher ranks out there, among the fighting angels. There were angels above him of much higher importance, whom he answered too.

He had a plaster on his nose, which made me think that he did get into fights all the time, but rather unwisely. He made a sign that he now had to leave, and I felt a sense of urgency rising up inside me. I pulled his arm, and insisted that he told me something too. 'What about me'? I asked him, and addressed a concrete problem. He said that the matter was not decided yet, and that he didn't know anything about it. While pulling away from me, and now looking very anxious, as if he was afraid that he may have crossed the higher powers, he told me that I had two options: 'Either you let 'them' work on it, or you intervene.' I made an attempt at holding on to him: 'Who is *them,* and how can I intervene?' But he was gone.

My father as a pirate in 1961, Romania

I have to say that this was one of the most powerful dreams I have ever had. It also had all the shamanic elements in it: The crossing over after meeting the gatekeeper in the shape of the wormwood woman, though this crossing did not go all the way, as the meeting with the spirit guide, my father, took place somewhere in between, at the house at the crossroads. During this meeting I was also conscious all the time that this was a dead person I was talking too, hence my insistence that he told me something significant. Even now I'm still thinking about what he said, and I'm still asking: Who is 'them'? Working on what exactly? Why does what I've asked to know still need working on at high level? And what about the potential danger, or maybe not, of my interfering? Why was my father under restriction to tell me more, and who was the other man piloting the UFO?

IT'S ALL IN THE CARDS

The day after this dream I performed a simple ritual of giving thanks. I wrote a poem for my father, lit a white candle, burned some wormwood, and recited power words. Such personal dreams that develop into full-fledged personal narratives can also be thought of as prompters for more storytelling work whose aim is to awaken us to possibilities we only dream of.

Connected to the dream above, yet after some time had passed, I performed a divination with the cards; just a reading in-line of five cards. Although I assigned a card for each of the different fragments of my dream that came in coherent manner – the arrival of the UFO, the wormwood woman, meeting my father, his message, and the overall impression – my reading took the form of a singular sentence.

As I went from the 3 of Batons to the 4 of Coins, then to the Star, the Empress and finally to the 10 of Coins, my sense of the literalness of my dream was transposed unto the cards. The propelling batons sending me to the square building to receive the gift of wormwood so that I could meet the one who joined the stars and who would tell me about myself and my potential to rule over a sack of money seemed like a solid reading to me. But why the 10 coins ending the string of cards? Hadn't I told the wormwood woman that I had no money to buy for myself the flying device? Or are the 10 coins a suggestion that the matter is sealed, even though some are still working on it? And why am I seeing the Empress's red nipple multiplied by 10 on the 10 coins? What is reflected here? Why is my father not represented in the cards as the tattooed pirate he showed himself as? Is it because, as he suggested, he occupies too low a rank in heaven to deserve an image on earth?

The Star suggests that our meeting took place under good auspices. The Empress suggests that I have agency and the power to reflect and act on what I'm doing. Coins are associated with female power. They get warm in our hands and we can cut deals with them. The only masculine force here is represented by the 3 batons, a sign of incremental power. A swirl into a road that cuts through two crossing options, leading to a place where gifts are received.

The dove offering a twig, the gift of wormwood, turns into an emblem on the Empress's shield. A pact has been made under the guiding stars. If the naked woman must don a dress, it will be a winged one. Something is definitely accomplished. Something tangible. Eight stars turn into eight coins. The ninth is the semilunar diadem, and the tenth the crown.

Coins can be most magical, buying secrets, act as a treasure, or function as talismans. The fixed star Spica in the constellation Virgo is often represented as a bird on a coin. Magicians of old would have this coin on them as one of their most treasured possession, as a sign of great fortune to be upon them.

STAR MAGIC RITUAL

From dreams we can derive a method for divination, or use the cards as prompters for talismanic magic. Based on the dream and the cards above, if I were to devise a necromantic ritual for accessing information from the dead, an ancestor, or a familiar spirit, I would do the following:

- Choose a clear night and create a sacred space in nature. A good place would be one that suggests descent into the underworld. A cave, a crypt, or one's own basement can also do.
- Light a candle.
- Burn some incense.
- Place an iron pot on four legs next to the candle, and fill it with water.

- Throw a silver coin inside it.
- Under the starry sky make some offerings in the form of libation poured directly into the ground.
- Make a strong and powerful invocation of royal command, calling ancestral spirits by their full name.
- Align 10 coins around the iron pot.
- Concentrate, and stare into the pot at the silver coin, and past the reflection of water.
- Allow for a portal to open. It is important that you give yourself time.
- Register all the sounds, images and impressions that come through the water.
- Articulate a concrete question or concern and wait for an answer to emerge.
- In closing, offer a prayer of thanks, and send spirit on its way.

AS ABOVE SO BELOW

As an alternative to the above ritual, I can refer the reader to the medieval grimoir, the Picatrix, where we read about one of the sciences of necromancy, 'the science of the image'. The Picatrix is basically a manual in stellar magic, instructing the sorcerer or the magician in the arts of drawing down astral power (trans. Greer and Warnock, 2010). Through the right invocations and suffumigations, exposing a talisman to incense, the sorcerer gains access to hidden knowledge, which the Picatrix defines as being part of any necromantic work, or the work of creating a magical image. In the Picatrix necromancy has a theoretical part, dealing with the power and movement of the stars, and a practical part, dealing with the infusion of the power of the fixed stars so that they cast their light on the planets they form a conjunction with.

The idea is to extract from the stars their power – a talisman literally means a violator – and 'force' them to shine through a sigil protective energy, or to manifest desires. According to the Picatrix, the stars can lend one's magic the quality of the three virtues that the grimoire identifies as the sub-lunar categories, ranging from the animal, to the mineral, and vegetable kingdom.

In principle, all magical operations can be considered alchemical insofar as they rely on finding the right ingredients to mix and then balance them properly. For example, I once consecrated my home made absinthe to the fixed star Algol when it was conjunct the dark Moon also conjunct the Sun. Not many want to approach this star, as it has a way of making heads disappear. In astrological cosmology Algol, Ras al Ghul, or the Demon Star, is the head of the Gorgon Medusa. Perseus decapitated her simply because she was a terrible monster, turning anyone who would gaze onto her into stone. Of course, Medusa was not always the maiden with hair made of serpents, and angry with all men. She used to be a beautiful woman in the temple of Minerva, but when she gave birth to Chrysaor and Pegasus by Neptune, Minerva didn't like it, hence she turned her into a demon.

In astrological parlance, whenever Algol is conjunct anything, you can be sure to experience a loss of heads, more often literally than merely metaphorically. But there are instances when Algol conjunct the Sun will give victory over one's enemies. We can all use that. In my magical understanding, however, there is no terrible power, or a power that's terrible enough to frighten us. As I have already remarked, power is power. It is neither good, nor bad. The best is to get a sense of how we can be in the proximity of power without losing our heads between our legs.

According to Agrippa and The Picatrix the herbs sacred to Algol are hellebore and mugwort. I made a smoke offering of that mix over Algol's image that I drew by hand at the exact moment when the star was applying to its conjunction point. As wormwood, the main ingredient in absinthe, is particularly good for dream work, the idea was not only to get on the wavelength with Algol's power, but also use Algol's light saber to cut through the hidden inessentials populating my unconscious.

As I was letting the incense fumes go to the ceiling of my den, aka the kitchen, I understood that there are certain powers that we can mix. That's the whole point of ritual. To get us to a place where we suddenly realize that we rather like our lives such as they are, and especially when they are not under dictations. For let's face it, how many would endorse any activities that are not consecrated by what the neighbor has to say? Most of the time we plod along, doing what there is to be done, and making sure we don't fall too much into cultural disrepute.

While enjoying this life that makes me think of stars and fumes, luminaries and planets sharing house with the greatest celestial female force – not that the mortals get that, what with most still being frightened of what women might be up to, disrupting the neat social order and such – I used the cards to consolidate my invocation. For this type of magic, as words must follow the act, it is crucial that we get them to resound a message that is aligned with both our conscious and unconscious desire. Our magical act must become part of our unconscious if it is to work at all, and it is for this reason that we place ourselves consciously in the service of image and word under smoke. And yet, whenever I use the cards in the creation of talismans, what attracts me to this ritual, which is quite commonsensical, is my appreciation of the way the cards seem to address a dimension that is above the magical act itself, insofar as they point to a meta-statement, that is to say, a statement about the function and quality of the cards themselves, before they spell out a message according to the context of the question or the intended purpose at hand.

To the extent that we can give ourselves license to talk about just how much more we get out of life when we walk the walk and talk the talk, I'll say this: I can never get tired of the perfection of the way the cards fall randomly on the table. I can never get enough of musing about just how much power there is in sitting there and contemplating The Sun, The Popesse, and The Devil presiding over my absinthe mix, as in the context above. The Popess mediating between the two heads, Medusa's heads before and after, knows what she knows. She gathers in her book the brilliance of the Sun, and the Devil's bidding. The Demon star shows up here too, saying, 'I'm here now. Ask me anything.'

What I got from the cards in this situation is a sense of dance with the twinkle of the star. Apart from composing my invocation, the cards were also enforcing for me that what I was doing was good, as my magical act was bringing me closer to experiencing perhaps the thing itself, the movement of the universe as it goes from contraction to expansion. The cards gave me a sense of my own place in the grander picture, and they created a concrete counterpoint to the image of Algol's hidden powers as inscribed in the old-age figure concentrated in the body-less head, the head that governs the blade and the pen, establishing once more the ultimate balance and justice: As above, so below.

Here I should mention that although I realize that many card readers prefer to consider the astrological correspondences imposed on the cards – a practice that became popular since the 60s – I do not find this approach useful. The stars and planets have an exact astronomical movement and cycle in relation to the observant eye from the perspective of the earth. Laying cards on the table at random is not the same as following the impact the planets make through casting a horary, electional, or natal chart. The Empress as Venus may be conjunct the Hermit or Saturn, on the table, but if Venus is up to something else, in the sky, then that's what I consider more significant.

If I choose to perform stellar magic, such as for instance placing the most fortunate fixed star, Spica, on the Ascendant, or conjunct one of the angular houses in the quadrant house system from Placidus to Regiomontanus – electing also the right moment when the 7 planets are fortunately aligned with the cusps of the houses that interest me for my purpose – I do not use the cards to map what is happening in the sky. What I do instead is erect an electional or horary chart which I then place against my natal chart and against the transits occurring at the exact moment when I let my fumes infuse Spica's sigil.

What I use the cards for is inspiration with my invocation, or as a door to how to go about stating what I wish in the best possible way. In this sense, while I allow my magic to follow astronomical and astrological rules and myths, I think of the cards as poetry, not cosmology. I think of the cards as the voice of my magic, uttering the words that invite the stellar power into my sacred space. I thus work simultaneously with what I can do myself through the medium of the cards at the interpretative level and with what the stars can do for me as a matter of grace. All I need to do about the latter is sit and wait patiently for good alignments to occur. It is precisely in this conflation of action with surrendering to proper time that I find other voices guiding me, whether they be those of the ancestors or those of the sky and the earth.

As the cards invite the stars to sing for me, the right time and the right fumes direct their light into my talismans. With these then I walk in balance.

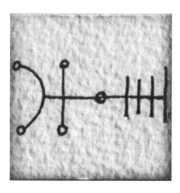

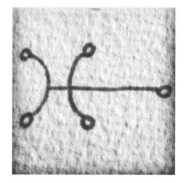

NECROMANCY

My father died, my mother died, my grandfather died at the tender age of 47, a mad man. There are many dead in my family, and many family secrets gone with them. While the dead have a way of being dead by virtue of anatomical disintegration, physically speaking they are still stardust. I like to think of the stars when I think of the dead, and how the stars can help us navigate through the realms of the wondrous liminal space between the worlds.

When my sister comes to visit me and I'm alone with my dog, we work. By this I mean that we do stuff that most people don't. What we are particularly good at is detective work. We dig into issues and concerns, but we don't stay put. We don't stop at what makes sense. We push forward and test our own limits of sensing and understanding. We cross hedges, bust boundaries, and laugh at the incredulous. This latter laughter is part of the program that we call: 'The fun the crazies have when they go against the rational.'

One night we decided to uncover an annoying family secret that, at least according to our genealogical sources, goes back to 1880. We started with a shamanic journey induced by two frame drums, a rattle, and a kissing She-Goddess Husky, Frigg. Each with her way. My sister is good with outer space capsules and a bathyscaphe, a free-diving self-propelled deep-sea submersible. I'm good with the Green Man and other such figures. Papa Legba showed the Vodou way, and before I knew it, after a tour in a Mongolian yurt filled with silk draperies that Papa invited me in, I found myself doing some carpentry, hammering nails into a coffin. When the drums went silent, my sister said: 'The bathyscaphe didn't work today, so it looks like we won't get to the bottom of this.' Not good. I started wondering about the significance of my coffin and the extent to which I contributed to sabotaging the very purpose of this work. Coffins are known to hold on to secrets, not reveal them.

We decided to try my very special antique crystal ball made for Two Worlds in Manchester in 1890. My sister is particularly good at scrying. I drummed some more, and at a new pace she started pouring out information. 6 people: 3 men and 3 women. Illegal love. A magician with white hair and a long cape, and an old hag with big watery eyes fixing something in the sky. A dead man with a moustache. A round sigil made out of two disks sealing a box, and a shadoof resembling very much the letter Y – as all ancient well-poles do.

Next we wanted to know how this secret affected us. We went for a simplified geomantic reading where we read just for one geome (we didn't use the full method for geomantic divination that makes recourse to various constellations).

Caput Draconis showed up, and my sister recited from the lore: 'You must use your right hand in good for good and evil for evil'. 'Fair enough,' I said. 'Let's cut the cards with the right hand then,' I further said, while holding a pack in my left hand and getting ready for concrete imagery. We needed to know who the people that showed up were. The only one who could be identified in the scrying was the hag. She was my paternal grandmother, a dead woman now, whom we last saw some 40 years ago. She was easy to identify, by her big eyes and flamboyant manner. Though not a gypsy, she used to wear flowing, large skirts and colorful headdresses, and she smoked the long pipes like a chimney. She was not what others would call a 'proper woman.' Indeed not. She knew things and took no dictations from anyone, least of all the patriarchs around her.

We proceeded with pulling cards at random, one for each of the figures that my sister saw in the crystal ball. Something was odd. Some of the male figures in the scrying session turned out as women in the cards, and some women turned out as men. Especially the dead mustached man as the Empress was interesting. (S)he was carrying a sigil on the shield all right, yet the card signifying the sigil itself in the scrying session showed up in the card of the Pope that we pulled specifically for it. We were happy with that. Just by looking at the Pope's disciples, and assessing their round hair-cuts, assured us that this card here was definitely the right one. My sister insisted that it was exactly those round shapes with another circle inside them that presented themselves, as if they were shaved coins.

We also thought that the shadoof and Caput Draconis were in cahoots, having the exact same shape, the shape of Y. The Sun and the Hermit gave us a pretty good idea as to what happened after the Star, as the cheating man, busted his own Tower, leaving a whole World behind in a hat. The first protagonist in the scrying session was an elegant woman with a hat on, so we decided that there was some good symmetry and rhyme between the hat in the Magician's hat in the scying and the mandorla in the World card. The hag had the Moon's eyes, which was understandable in this context, and the Magician, now turned Charioteer, looked like he took off victoriously in his carriage after the deed was done.

All this made perfect sense to us. But we needed to know what was placed in the scales, as it was obviously not for nothing that we got a fountain pole showing up in the crystal. I put a new card down, and voilà, Justice. The scale in the scale? A secret inside another secret? This was beginning to look more like the

kind of poetry that you don't understand, but for whatever reason you are sure that you like it. This told us that something was
definitely weighed. Was the dead man weighed and found want-
ing? And who was the judge?

At this point we got the chills, and while our hair was rising,
the dog decided to be in a more cheerful and greeting mode: It
shot for the door and started barking like a maniac – and odd occurrence, as Huskies are not in the habit of barking. We were not
expecting any guests at 11.30 pm, so who was there? 'I'm not so
sure it's the dead one,' my sister said. We pulled a card: The Fool.
'Ah, I said, 'it's Papa Legba, he has a thing for sigils and coming
through doors.' 'Fair enough,' my sister said, and then insisted on
having a look at his vévé.

Lastly we wanted to know what the dead had to tell us about this secret. After all, you don't get to show up in a reading like this for nothing, both as a woman, when you're a man, and with all the regalia and initials on your dead chest. We pulled the card of the Popesse, or the High Priestess. 'Look at that,' my sister said, delivering a tirade: 'I told you we were not going to get to the bottom of this. The lips of this handsome mustached man are sealed. And what business did you have hammering those nails in that coffin? We are not going to know anything now.' I pulled a last card: The Force, or Strength. I then said to her: 'Listen, we just have to insist.' 'Yes,' she said, 'but these forces make my hair rise, and besides, when the ghost came in we forgot to say welcome. We're ignorant.' 'That we are,' I said, 'but is this also a reason to be afraid?' 'I guess not,' she said, and then went thoughtful – or was it rational, they call it?

We decided to spill some libation for all, and then have ourselves a good midnight beer before going to bed, courtesy of the Danish Brewery called Amager and a very generous friend who knows that my favorite pale ale is the one called Wookiee.

I made an attempt at staying up longer. 'But there was that thing about the Magician. His black umbrella.' 'Nice try,' my sister said. 'I'm not going to fall for it. We'll be analyzing nothing no more tonight.' She went to bed, and I took it upon myself as a diligent scribe to record faithfully what else one can do with one's Tarot cards besides reading them according to nice little positional spreads. So here is a reflection:

All you need for magical work is a few sacred tools. These will only be as sacred as you make them. Do you breathe words of power into them? They will whisper powerful messages back at you. Bring in a gatekeeper, a crystal ball and geomancy, and you're set for adventure. If some family secret resists you, at least you can get to plan your next detective move. Has anybody mentioned Sherlock Holmes in a movie with that dashing Robert Downey Jr. in it? While putting pen to paper in recording this event, I was tempted to send a letter to Hollywood. For a moment there, I was convinced that I could write much better stories for the screen. Not to mention true ones. But some personal stories may have to stay that way.

The point of this story here is to emphasize also the very pragmatic scope of any magical working beyond its intended function, which, in my case, is the sheer pleasure of enjoying the company of my sister without having to go through the banality of recounting frustrations related to the reality of our 'normal' lives, mine often consisting of complaints about the stupidity of educational reforms within the academy, devoid of any substance, and hers related to her clinical psychology approach and work at the hospital that often lacks basic common sense and empathy.

In our encounters we have also found that raving about our achievements, or those of our loved ones, is only interesting for about 3 seconds. Hence, we have long since realized that the best of ourselves together is found in our letting sacred objects not only mediate between us, but also inform all our gatherings. Nothing really compares to the work of blessing our own treading on this planet, and making recourse to unusual practical magic behavior that enhances our awareness of alternative modes of viewing the world. A community of two can work marvels.

Working with the cards in a magical setting – whether for divination or for influencing the patterns of mainstream conduct – has the advantage of making us aware of what we have forgotten, often how to use our body and our most basic senses. Whenever we do something with magical intent, the most crucial sense to activate besides seeing is hearing and smelling. For me, smelling kicks in first. When magic is aloof, I start smelling something that's usually odd, or very strong, or out of the ordinary. That's how I know that I've crossed a threshold. That's when I start making myself extremely vigilant, which is to say that I start paying attention to everything. I start listening much more intently to my surroundings. I question my ability to register the magical world around me in a tactile way. Can I touch what I 'see', and how does it feel? Is my taste present too?

A trained magician will have all her senses activated, but to being with, I think that hearing and smelling are very good friends. If we pay attention, we might just discover that our senses bring us to the right magical place. Once there we will know what to do, and for what purpose exactly.

The point of working magic with the cards, or other consecrated, devotional objects, is to get a sense of how clarity takes
shape beyond the first, literal level of interpretation. The idea is
to see how this clarity then manifests itself in the exegetic, or
hidden level of symbolic meaning, so that we ultimately can utter
not only 'I knew it', but also realize that the symbol is not always
all there is.

NO MAGIC

Most students of the occult arts who learn to read cards don't think that what they are practicing is divination and prediction, psychology and sorcery, all at the same time. As far as I'm concerned I make no distinction between these strands, although, as history has demonstrated, some have always been interested in drawing the line between predictive methods and consultancy, whether it be within the context of laying down three cards to advise a soul on a love matter or waking up the dead to help one speculate on the money market. Indeed, the line is thin between suggesting to someone, upon seeing the trio of The Star, The Magician and The Sun, that all they need in order to get the significant other is a splash of beautifying the body by taking a bath in rose water while allowing the other to play voyeur, and merely suggesting that they need more confidence. For how would this confidence come about, and how would it manifest? As an abstract thing in one's psyche, because that's what the 'intuitive' card reader has said?

Some would call the latter approach in my example a more neutral form of helping a soul in need of self-confidence, as it makes recourse to reminding the person to love herself first. But in fact, if the advice is to be effective at all, then it needs to be followed by creating a concrete picture for the other to relate to, so that a complete understanding of the act of seduction is possible. 'You want this man? Show him your nakedness and hit it off with him without any regard for consequences', would be my advice, if I saw the cards above in the context of a question on how to best go about attracting the other.

But obviously this is more risky business than if I were to merely tell the person to be more confident, as spelling the action out involves the kind of approach that may not always be endorsed by society at large. What if the person I told this to comes from a culture where sex before marriage is not an option? As history has also shown, the courageous fortuneteller has always run the risk of getting herself stoned. Nowadays the rejection of wizards and sorcerers has translated into a counter-rejection, with the wizards and sorcerers being more concerned with ethics than with magic. It's safer that way. 'What the person needs to do has to come from herself,' some would say, but what exactly would that be? Some seekers go home with the same merry-go-round of not knowing. While I get the implication of what needs to come out from within, seen from the point of view of clinical psychology as it is consecrated by the institution, I don't get the point of it if I want to perform an efficient act of magic based on blending symbolic action and intent with the power of suggestion.

For me, magic is not about following uncritically either a specific tradition or giving in to the fear that what we're doing may not be proper in relation to the so-called free will of another. The only thing that interests me in my work with the cards is efficiency and common sense. When I read the cards and perform magic I do it in accordance with paying attention to what is needed, not in accordance with second-guessing.

One of my favorite contemporary horary astrologers, John Frawley, has this to say, implicitly suggesting that we stop worrying too much about what we call magic, how we perform it, and to what end; and focus instead on action.

> Our rational world claims to have swept magic quite away; but it is not, however, such a stranger to us as we may think. Our days are filled with what we believe are magical actions. I drink this brand of cola to make myself sexy; drive that marque of car to fill my life with glamour and adventure. If I think of my true love and burn a candle in front of a statue of Venus, I am performing an overtly magical action; if I present my true love with a bunch of roses (ruled by Venus) or a box of chocolates (ruled by Venus) my action is none the less magical for being apparently ordinary. I am plying her with Venus, as it were, seeking by sympathetic magic to raise her "Venus-levels" to a point where she finds me irresistible. The scientific sceptic may deny the efficacy of magic, but he still does not arrive on his girl-friend's front porch carrying a cabbage. (Frawley, 2001: 159)

In addition to this common sense I would say the following as well[1]: Magic is making something out of nothing. But this cannot happen unless you prime your mind to something first. Let us call this something 'tradition.' This means that if you can see it, it exists. Priming your mind to seeing demons or angels is working with fiction. You need fiction in order to get to the significant and

---

1   This fragment has appeared in 'Return to Mago'. Magoism.net. July, 7, 2015.

workable 'nothing'. If magic didn't come out of nothing, it would not be magic. It would be 'tradition' alone.

If magic works it is not because you read some formula in an old book, but because you allow for the fiction in your head to let 'nothing' pass through. If magic were not 'nothing', it would be borrowing. Without 'nothing' magic is other people's claims; it is their thoughts, not yours. Without 'nothing' magic is impersonal. Without the personal magic is nothing, where 'nothing' here means highlighting the unsuccessful operation.

We need tradition as tradition primes our minds to the 'something' that helps us with our workings, whether for a spell, conjuration, communion with the forces of nature, or more modestly, reading cards. But we also need more than tradition. Tradition means using a system of thought or a method that will get you going, or that will put you on your path. But what is this path, or where exactly is it that we are going, the self-proclaimed magicians of the world? The good magician moves towards 'nothing' because it is in this very nothing that she gets a sense of what she can do 'outside' of the tradition or the teachings that she has been through. Anything else is stealing, being worth something because your master is worth something, or having a name because your master has a name. This is called being able to perform half-magic. The magician that relies on tradition alone for her workings is half the magician her master is. A good magician is the magician who, when she snaps her fingers, talks to nothing. She asks 'nothing' to assist her in her working as this working in the 'nothing' is unmediated by dogma, influence, or by second-guessing the master. The magician who uses tradition alone, and has never travelled to the land of 'nothing', has neither courage nor imagination.

Now, what is this nothing? I identify this 'nothing' with 'the thing itself'. You can learn to ride with Death by snapping your fingers every time you travel to the so-called upper world, in shamanic parlance – as a good friend of mine does – but if the snapping of the fingers doesn't put you right there at the core of the thing itself, then you're merely imagining things, not experiencing them. You can do magic theoretically, or in principle, or because you strongly believe in your grimoire, but it still amounts to nothing, 'nothing' here in the sense of your magic being worthless. Magic that comes to you by way of tradition alone, and without the 'nothing' of the thing itself and which is not the 'something' of your tradition, is even less than half-magic. It is no magic at all. Just an insistence on your own low self-esteem. An insistence on not knowing what you do know. A claim to a connection that is not even your own.

You can only use tradition to say NO to it. You must learn tradition so that you can be adamant in saying NO to it. This NO is part of the magic of NOthing. Without this NO your magic is a stale preservation, a tin can where you safe-keep your master's bones.

Magic is detachment from being concerned with what people think of you, especially what other magicians think of you. When we say, 'do your own thing' we mean 'do your nothing'. This nothing is your very backbone, your spine and stamina, your triumph over tradition and the witch that came before you. This nothing is also the ultimate way of connecting with your masters. You honor their 'something' for you with your own 'nothing'. If you can achieve your own 'nothing', you get to the thing itself. That's the ultimate magic: To perform your own thing, and not what any tradition dictates. Anything else is a pathetic cry for attention. A fumbling. Fear of not being good enough.

But merely being good enough is not good enough at all. You must be sovereign in magic. In your strong, sovereign magic you are above tradition. You refer to tradition, and point your little finger to it, and you can even wear an elegant glove, but you must do more than perform. The function of drama and costume is to make you and everything you hide behind it transparent. The magician that's above tradition is not transparent. The magician that's above tradition works with all the four major elements at once. She moves everything with her breath. Together they are beyond negotiation. There's no settling for merely 'good enough'. Together, fire, water, air, and earth – which the magician also embodies – acknowledge each other's sovereignty, and in that equilibrium the thing itself emerges out of nothing. Tradition can't compete with that. Tradition teaches, but 'nothing' achieves.

I am a magician of NOthing. I work with the thing itself, and this is way better than good enough, better than any tradition that is itself only an invention. I aim for magic of the most perfect caliber. My magic is my butterfly in my gun. Funk and Wagnall's *Standard Dictionary of Folklore, Mythology and Legend* tells us that with a butterfly in your gun you can't possibly miss the target. That's right. This is an old superstition. I take what's good from it. But how I get my gun to hit that target by using what tradition prescribes, namely the putting of a butterfly in the mouth of the gun, is based entirely of my centering on nothing. 'What is your place?', I ask myself, and I can decide that my place is among the best shotguns in the world, perhaps because I've had good schooling. But that is only good enough. If I can decide that my place is in the opening of the gun itself, where the butterfly sits, then I can achieve something that I can call magic. Without such trespassing of rules – 'hold your gun like this and press it like this with your finger' – and without transgression – 'but I want to stick my own head in the line of fire' – there's only superstition. And who needs that? Who needs to waste their time explaining again and again what the function of tradition is vis-à-vis any magical working?

Magic is the act of disobeying tradition while being able to spell tradition's name in your name.

THE DEAD SPEAK THE TRUTH

'So then, nobody died?', I asked the person in front of me, coming for what she referred to as a touch of necromancy. Although I insist on calling what I do with the cards 'reading the cards', it is true that on occasion, by virtue of the questions I get, we could argue that I can easily end up reading more than the cards. So be it.

'Nobody died yet, but it feels as if they died,' she said. Fair enough. I know that feeling.

'So, what are we then looking for?,' I asked.

'We're looking for a third-hand insight,' she said, giving me the squinting look. I know that one too. And I have to admit that I like it. There's nothing like reading for third parties, or 'third-hand insights'.

'What do you want to know?'

'Once a person I loved declared me dead. But he knows as well as I know that with a connection like ours such a death is not possible. I want to know what he was afraid of.

'I know this knowledge too. So, then, you're dead?' I insisted.

'In a manner of speaking,' the woman said. 'I want to know about the bond.'

'Ok, this is getting interesting,' as said, 'for, in a manner of speaking, you call yourself up from the dead to speak the truth.'

'Yes,' she said while I was shuffling the cards.

'Here we go: you got 8 of cups, the Devil, 7 of cups.

'Ah,' the woman said, staring at the center card.

'Yes,' I said, 'the bond is there. You may have been vanquished to the underworld, but the bond is there. The 8 of cups together with the Devil testify to a form of tender obsession. It would have been a lot worse with the 8 of swords. The 2 cups in the middle of the first card turn into the two imps under the Devil's control. The Devil makes a gesture for the third cup in the middle of the last card to be conjoined with the others. Perhaps you were declared dead because your lover feared for his most precious. What did he hold precious?'

'I can't tell you, but it is more than his name.'

'Your lover was afraid of bondage. He was hoping to get out of the bundle, and perhaps like the single cup in the middle of the last card, enjoy standing alone in the free space. But there's a reason why traditionally the 7 of cups has been associated with a troubled heart. The single cup taking center stage may be enjoying the attention from the others, but it is alone. It is not exactly on the same page with the others, even though it's of the same kind. This is the kind of situation that says: I'll be damned if I do, and I'll be damned if I don't.

'So, what you're saying, then, is that I'm the Devil?'

'In a manner of speaking, but forget not that to begin with there's equality. There's also equality in the Devil card, if we agree that the 2 cups rhyme with the 2 imps, so neither you of you rules over the other here. The single cup in the last card rhymes with the Devil himself. So perhaps the man feared becoming the Devil himself. And yet he declared death to you. This means that you are both the Devil and the dead'.

'Ah, that makes a lot more sense, the woman said, so I'm the dead and the Devil at the same time.'

'Exactly,' I said, and concluded that this particular 'necromantic' session had the flavor of the eternal return.

ACCOUNTING

The point that I'm trying to make with these examples is that, more often than not, we see magic emerge in the very pattern of the cards, even before we set out to practice any. Symmetry is magical, and so is the rhyming scheme of the elements dancing from one card to the next, transforming their form and function. The cards following some simple principles of magical thinking can teach us about the value of action and choice. Let me illustrate again:

In her works on the natural numbers, *Number and Time* and *Psyche and Matter*, Gustav Jung's assistant, Marie-Louise Von Franz recounts the story of the value of numbers for the Chinese. Even in the military, where men of logic and order rule, it looks like action and choice are under the law of qualitative numbers rather than quantitative ones. So, once upon a time there were eleven generals who had to decide whether to go to war or not. They took a vote. Three were in favor, eight against. They went to war. Now the question: What must these men have been possessed by to engage, following the minority, when the majority decided against it unambiguously?

According to the Chinese tradition of assigning more symbolic value to some numbers over others, a relation of worth taking precedence over success becomes crystal clear: Insofar as the number three expresses unanimity, and number eight indicates dubious attachments, it follows logically to endorse the three and discard the eight. This story makes one think of Einstein's often quoted line: 'Try not to be men of success but men of value,' which allows us to ditch our foolish urge to only engage with things that 'make sense.'

Von Franz also wrote a fascinating commentary to a medieval text attributed to Thomas Aquinas, *Aurora Consurgens.* In Aquinas's 'Fourth Parable On the Philosophic Faith which Consisteth in the Number Three,' there is an interesting relation of sublimated value between eternity, equality, and the bond between eternity and equality. Diverting the energy associated with 'unacceptable' impulses into a socially acceptable activity has only the function of getting it wrong. While Von Franz makes the obvious remark that 'the entire work of the alchemists is an endeavor to reintegrate that unsublimable residue, the sinners on earth and the fallen angels, into a whole' (255), we are left to ponder on why we love the logic of action as dictated by symbolic choice.

The other point I want to make is that I use the cards either for practical or more abstract concerns, without, however, making a distinction between the ways in which I approach the cards. Cards are cards. In my opinion you can divine with anything, and with any cards. It's all in the method and the question you pose. I can pose wisdom questions to a door, or a cabinet with many drawers, or a line of trees, or a monogram on a handkerchief. That's the beauty of divination. That it can turn any ordinary object into an extraordinary tool, a life saver, a magical accounting for life.

The card reader, or the fortuneteller, while relying on a system of transmission, often arrives at her 'truth' in that unmediated form that is specific to all working oracles. For what is magic indeed, if not the ability to detach yourself from what your neighbor thinks of you? By the same token, we can say that a good fortuneteller moving beyond divination to performing magic with the cards is very little concerned with what the witch that came before her did and how she did it.

A good fortuneteller is one who is grounded in her own privately arrived at connection with the cards, spirit, the devil, light, or demons, or whatever works for her. Personally, therefore, I'm always very suspicious of all who claim lineage and an ability to stick to some purported rules only. Such nonsense. Knowing history is a good idea, and coming from a family known for its folk-magic skills is a great gift, but if history is all one does as a fortuneteller, that is not enough for magical working that's efficient. Also, having a gift is not the same as working it. I happen to know folks who 'have it', as others put it when referring to magical inheritance, but who either deny it, suppress it, or downright let it pass due to indulgence and negligence. Thus, it is not history or personal history that makes us good at the magical interpretative and performing arts, but rather the ability to see through it like we would through the dense matter of this earth we all tread upon.

I have come to learn that the reason why some insist on dogma that they ultimately invent themselves, but which they claim comes from ancient sources, is the classical reason. People don't trust themselves to know what they know. What does this mean? This means that they don't have enough confidence in how strong their working is. Why don't magicians know how strong their working is? For the simple reason that they don't have a well-rounded and grounded connection.

A strong connection is established through a willingness to work with nature as it exceeds our grasp. This involves a quieting of our mental capacity in favor of allowing nature to speak to us through the senses that we don't use too often: Hearing, smelling, touching, moving, dancing to the music our words can make.

THE PATH OF MAGIC

*Poetic creation still remains an act of perfect spiritual
freedom.
Poetry remakes and prolongs language; every poetic
language begins by being a secret language.*

– Mircea Eliade, *Shamanism*

The point of magic is to un-perplex us. Magic is simple. Magic
is play. All it takes is to designate and to nominate. Create relations that will get you there where you walk the web of connections, and where you not only perform, but also embody what
you state. And it doesn't even matter if you hit a wall, or create
one on purpose because you don't want to say what you have to
say directly. If your intention is addressed to a specific other, even
when the performance of the enunciation takes place in a vacu-
um, it will still work. In fact, it will create an even stronger bond,
as this enunciation will fall on an abstract plane that is devoid of
personal investment. As they say, beware whom you address in
the void. There may be eyes there, watching and responding to
the wish for fulfillment.

The eyes have a penetrating function. The ears are receptive. You cast an informed glance, things happen. That is to say, you can make a clock stop, or cause a migraine in another if you can conjure enough possessive power, or enough will that will enable you to not only distinguish, but also own whatever force that moves from blessing to cursing. Your eyes can cast your envy, jealousy or possessiveness unto another. They call it casting the evil eye. Your eyes can also bless and cure. They can imagine weaving square knots in front of your body, or that of another, protecting against derailed flow and imbalance.

How do we do this? What path are we walking when we consciously provoke distress? Or when we realize that now we bring comfort to ourselves and others in one way or another, whether physically or mentally felt? The magical path is often perplexing to the young magician who must learn that just as she can consciously cast a gaze that's powerful enough to kill a tree, she can also use the same power to heal.

Once upon a time, to cure me of the worst fever ever, my father used an enchantment based on burning three matches into a glass of water, over which he said a special prayer. He made me drink that water, and accept the sign of the cross in a circle that he made on my forehead. I wouldn't have resisted anyway. I was too little and too ill. I was about four.

This is one of the very few, and earliest memories that I have. I can still remember the smell of that water, of burnt sulfur. I can also remember that no medical doctor could fix me. In my haze at the time, sounds have imprinted themselves onto my mind. I can still hear the rushed steps in and out of the emergency rooms and ambulance. But my father's dis-enchantment did it. The release. He was convinced that the evil eye was cast upon me. And he was right. A logical, medical solution was not enough to fix a magical problem. Other people have used similar remedies. Some say that it's good to take a herbal bath, or soak in a tub filled with beer and sea salt, if unwanted energy puts you in a place where you don't want to be.[1]

The un-perplexed wisdom when performing any kind of magic – whether ceremonial, conjuring spirits and the like, high and learned style, or folk magic, administering flying ointments or herbs or coal, low and humble style – is acknowledging the fact that while time must not be wasted, the mystery of what we're doing remains: In magical time, even what you don't say can be heard by those attuned to rhythm and vibration; those of the otherworld – and by the otherworld I mean a mode of experiencing a reality that is not informed by normative cultural precepts, but rather by a shift in our consciousness towards registering alternative modes of perception. There's consecration, to be sure, of the ritual that becomes a poetic act, but such consecration is given as a gift, not as spirit. What regulates the flow of spirit is faith, so the balance must be struck there, between faith and figure. As the magician embodies her tools, such as her cards, totem animals, the plants she is working with, or the elements, she not only works with invoking their power, but also becomes the thing itself: The wind, or water, the Popesse, or the Emperor, the Butterfly, or Mugwort.

Related to the anxieties that can arise from thinking about what one is doing, I often come across questions that pertain to one's own personal, magical path. Magicians, sorcerers, witches,

1 See particulary the classic manual of folk magic enchantments, *Spiritual Cleansing: Handbook of Psychic Protection,* and *Practice of Magic,* written by Draja Mickaharic (Weiser Books, 1985, 1995).

and shamans, can feel very ambivalent about what they claim, and if they do claim something, then they want to how they can own what they claim. 'How can I be sure of my path?', they all want to know.

Often the answer that fixes one's ambivalence is found within the intensity experienced in the connection to our subtle realities, the world of natural and stellar spirit, or the otherworld. To me, these are names we give to the distinction between technical magic, something we can all learn, and elective magic, something we experience on the basis of an election. Tradition has it that while many can practice forms of magic, not all 'are' magic, in the sense of experiencing having been elected to the craft, either by spirit or blood transmission. Usually if such an election occurs, then the one elected will know it by virtue of what is experienced: often resistance, illness, significant dreams, soul flights, or some other kind of torment that runs counter to one's established social and spiritual life.

Most of the literature describing shamanism, from the academic to the autobiographical, is filled with examples of how the magician is called to the task, and what kind of initiations may have to be undergone, before saying 'yes' to magic consolidates the new pact and path.[2] When magic exceeds the performative show – often a necessary condition for make-belief that the recipients of magic or spectators need in order to value what is going on – it becomes 'supernatural,' in the sense that it can elicit instant relief for an illness or distress. In this sense – magic as control, or ego involvement, plus magic as surrender, or ego renunciation – is more experiential than mechanical. The art is to

---

2 See the seminal work by historian of comparative religion, Mircea Eliade, *Shamanism: Archaic Technics of Ecstasy* (Princeton University Press, 1964).

have in equal measure the capacity to control one's act of surrendering and the capacity to reverse the act. The ability to cross thresholds is one skill, yet another skill altogether is required when you also have to come back; not dissimilar to the starting point, but different, as the return is very much contingent on what kind of guidance is given, which cannot be anticipated.

LEFT HAND OR RIGHT HAND PATH

But what is this path that can lead us to experiencing crossing the hedge, and once there, what exactly is it that we can perform? And what if the magician is required to perform something that goes against her ethical beliefs? While this would be the type of questions that the experienced magician never has to pose to herself, unless she wants a 'reality' check now and then, it is not so easy with the new ones approaching the way of life that requires a complete amnesia from what cultural pre-conditioning dictates. On this, I find that an efficient way of receiving immediate insight is to simply ask your cards about it. Let them guide you to an understanding.

Here is an example of a reading I once performed for a young sorceress, who posed this very question:

Which path is more suitable for me?
The left hand path or the right hand path?

In the parlance of magical discourse this question refers to what others have identified as black magic and white magic. I'm not so keen on making any such distinctions myself, as I see magic simply dealing with power, and not with the methods we devise to make use of this power. But I like to answer such questions for the sake of the structural contrast and symmetry that the cards often present us with.

As it happens, the cards here were quite blunt, yet in the final analysis they also suggested that one must make up one's mind as to who is to call the shots on making the final decision to walk, either this side, or the other side of magical practice.

I did a three-card reading for each situation:

On the **left hand path** we found the following:

The Pope, Justice, the Devil

On the **right hand path** we found the following:

The Lovers, The Magician, Judgment

How do we read these cards if we take the literal context of the question into consideration? It is as if the cards show an exact description of what we're dealing with at hand:

Black magic belongs to the realm of the Devil.

White magic belongs to the realm of the Angel.

Or so they say.

Here, it becomes crucial to understand what the sorceress wants to begin with: To be in cahoots with the Devil, and do what there is to be done in terms of pacts and bonds, or to mediate relations between the ambivalent subject (herself included) and the public?

Whereas the Devil invites us to the underworld, asking us to start with confronting our own demons, the Angel says, 'all rise, and let us now hear the news.'

Whereas in the first example we clearly have a situation that requires a complete cut (Justice) with the dogma of the mainstream church (Pope), and entering a formal submission to the

Lord of Darkness (Justice + Devil), the second example demonstrates a need to rise above the very idea of choice (Lovers) by tricking oneself (Magician) into believing that the sharing of higher learning is possible (Judgment).

Whereas in the first example, describing the left hand path, we are asked to consider giving up a pound of our own flesh and blood in exchange for magical knowledge (Justice cuts and weighs), the second example, for the right hand path, shows us that we are dependent on the community to acknowledge our magic. Moreover here, as the Magician is looking at the options on his table, we are meant to understand that he may not be aware of how much of that doubting of himself he ends up carrying into the new world.

Whereas the first example may involve working with necromancy, the ancestors, or the spirit of the telluric forces, the last example emphasizes work with the celestial forces as received by the larger group. If the first example shows us the transmission of personal gnosis, the price being going down, the second example shows us the transmission of group mentality, the price being having to listen up.

SUITABILITY

Now, let's go back to the question of suitability. Which one of these magical paths is more suitable for our sorceress?

Firstly, the answer to this question must be given in the preference for the particular practice that each of these three-card sequences describes ever so clearly. Secondly, the cards show us how agency is always in our own hands. If you're ready to enter a relation of exchange – you pay for your magical lunch – then you can expect the Devil to do your bidding when you need it. In the last example, while you're free to rise to the occasion or not, if you do rise, you'll need the community to pay for your magical lunch, and then, well, be ready to serve, for as they say, there is no free lunch.

While the first example may be good for the solitary witch and working with individual power, the second may be good for the ones who like group power, and working with circles of people.

CULTURE

Now, let us make clear that these divisions are culturally determined, and that if we run when we see the Devil, then it is probably because of the irrational fear instilled in us all by the grand religions of the world, having an agenda that has little to do with what I like to call natural magic.

This being the case, one then needs to also assess to what extent one can live with the cultural labels and epithets that the society at large will be more than ready to bestow on what one is doing. It may well be a good idea in this sense to ask oneself: Why is working with the 'Devil' condemned, while working with the 'Angel' is consecrated? Which camp do I want to be in? The winners or the losers?

Bear in mind that I'm still talking from the perspective of the society and what the society is ready to do to people who transgress the rules of the society. Now, this transgressive lunch is not too pretty, and history has it that good folks have been burned for a lot less than this discussion here.

THE THING ITSELF

On the occasion of this reading above, I was quite grateful to the cards for spelling out what is at stake in walking a particular path. This reading made me think that I salute the courageous ones, if they go with the Devil, for they will have shown determination and a willingness to live with 'the crazy.' But I also salute the ones who choose the Angel, for they can also perform work that is needed in terms of how we negotiate our place within the larger community. And then I salute the ones who can do both, for they will have said: 'My rising is above myself and all the others. I walk whichever path that is before me without thinking of any consequences.'

POWER

Questions about magic are questions about power. The bottom line is related to our willingness to explore raw power, or by contrast, the wisdom to explore what can be done when mediation is the pay-off. When looking at the cards, many would see the Magician as precisely that, a Magician, but in truth, no Magician is better than the Devil. The Magician in the Tarot is the cultivated man, the con man, or the fast strategist. He can get there, to the real power, but certainly not because he happens to be clever. Powerful magic has little to do with our calculations. Powerful magic begins with the act of surrendering. It begins with our controlling the extent to which we can tell ourselves, and act accordingly: 'Now I surrender'. Raw power à la the Devil is not for everyone. It requires courage and honesty, and a committed hunt for the truth.

Raw power is dangerous when it lacks proper channeling. It is not for nothing that, say, the Vodouists allow for full possession only in a ritual, communal setting. As not everyone can anticipate and know who will take over their bodies, with the consequence of loss of control over one's full conscious and acts, who is to prevent the embodied spirit from going amok? The last thing one needs are the law enforcement officers at one's door telling one gently, or not so gently, that now one will be locked up for a very long time.

In other shamanic circles there's therefore a strong insistence on instructing everyone that one never lose foothold of 'this' world. One foot here, one foot there, but never both feet over there. As with everything, the art is in finding the good balance, and in knowing exactly what one is doing while one is inviting raw power to take over. This may sound like a contradiction in terms, given that one must acquire quite some knowledge and experience before one allows for power to go through one unhindered, thus allowing one to experience something very basic, yet forgotten, namely a deep connection to all things. But then, this may yet be part of the way in which we define the excitement in magic: Without paradox, there's no magic.

Generally, when I speak about commending the one who can walk both paths, or indeed whichever path is laid before her, step on the left hand path with equal skill as she might step on the right hand path, I'm assuming already that the person in question actually knows what she is doing. Without that knowledge – whether arrived at by means of personal gnosis, books, or mentoring – there's only one option, namely getting lost in the woods.

Normally we don't commend people for their acts, if we see that they lack common sense. Also as a general rule here, it helps to know what one is good at. If one knows that, then chances are that one will also know which path is suitable for one's needs. Discernment lies at the heart of self-knowledge.

In my work with people for magical awareness, when I devise tailored programs for each individual according to a set of principles that works for me, I always begin with the telluric forces, as I know that these will work for them. 'Know thy earth', is my mantra here, for it is true that ashes go to ashes. 'Get a sense of the telluric first,' I then say, 'and you will see what magic comes to you.' The magical path goes through the belly of the earth. On her first walk through it, the magician receives poetic language, and with it the power to make the necessary invocations for all her magical performances.

The magical path is thus one of prolonged poetic language that depicts us all as connectors to the stars and the dust that went into our creation. As soon as we remove ourselves from cultural pre-conditioning, we stumble over the necessity of poetry. But this is not the kind of poetry that caters to our individual self-expression, often manifested as self-conscious cleverness about our ability to use words of power. What the otherworld shows us is the kind of poetry that speaks a secret language.

For this alone, walking the magical path is worth the while.

MAGICAL MORALS

Many cunning folk and witches operated out of a fundamentally monistic and animistic belief system. They therefore did not believe it necessary to be morally pure – in the Christian sense of the term – in order to enter mystical states and gain mystical knowledge and power, and they did not believe it necessary that their familiar spirit exhibit, or promote, moral purity in order to facilitate this transcendence.

– Emma Wilby, *Cunning Folk and Familiar Spirits*

Almost all contemporary books describing magical consciousness, whether scholarly or mainstream, tackle the issue of morality in magic. The premise for these discussions is often the distinction between white magic and black magic, high magic dealing with celestial beings, and low magic dealing with demons, light and dark forces, reading cards for divination or intervention. To the historians and anthropologists describing folklore magic, I prefer the scholars cum practitioners, as they tend to use their neutrality in an experiential way. This enables them to position themselves beyond describing binary oppositions, and adopt an attitude that is more inclusive. For instance, anthropologist

Susan Greenwood's practice of both high and low magic discloses what she makes of the magician's strategies of power when she evaluates what is at stake in assessing how magic relates to ethics and morality. Thus she states:

> The practice of magic can, in certain circumstances, legitimate what is perceived to be socially unethical or immoral behavior, in the name of higher power. (Greenwood, 2000: 179-180)

Emphasizing how the different worldviews on magic inform the practice of magic within or without codes of morality, Greenwood points out the fact that there are basically two modes of thinking that either accommodate or refute the 'dark' side of the otherworld. Her claim is that while the main religions such as Judeo-Christianity and Islam tend to be dualistic in their magical beliefs, stressing the Angel/Demon dichotomy, Paganism, and some forms of witchcraft are monistic, incorporating evil into a larger totality akin to the idea of connecting oneness that we find in Eastern philosophies, such as Hinduism and Buddhism (181).

Without going into the larger debate, and looking at the paradoxical states that arise from dogmatically going against dogmatic formulations that stress individual freedom – such as we may find them in the writings of Aleister Crowley, or in the Rede of the Wiccan credo: 'An it harm none, do as thou wilt,' I want to make a quick point that might inspire others to think about what they are saying when they utter the words 'magic and morality,' or when they express concern about the potential lack of morality in magical workings.

While I have been fortunate enough to have undergone some training in the magical arts with people who know what they are doing, I have to admit that I have always been suspicious of the warning to stay on my turf when performing magic, rather than intervening with other people's *wyrd* – for generally speaking, it is not very nice to impose your will on another person's will.

Here, I just want to pose this question: To what extent can we talk about ethics, my will against other people's will, criminal magical acts of sorcery, healing, and so on, once the hedge is crossed? As far as I can see, once the bridge to the otherworld is crossed, then you've left your own turf behind already. You are at the mercy of the otherworld, and the condition for your magical workings there is that you must assume whatever responsibility is laid on your shoulders. If you cannot do that, then it is perhaps best if you refrained from calling yourself a magician.

Also, insofar as in the otherworld there are no distinctions that are similar to the ones we make here in our mundane lives – as to the effect of what is good and what is bad for us, and so on – it is rather pointless to maintain the same system of values and hierarchies in the magical world as we do here, in our mainstream reality. Upholding normative codes and values devised according to our societal rules and conventions in the otherworld seems to defy the whole purpose with crossing thresholds. A magical world is a magical world, not a world of magic where good and evil is just better than the good and evil in this world.

In her work, *Cunning Folk and Familiar Spirits,* referred to here by way of the epigraph, Emma Wilby stresses how, in the shamanic visionary traditions in early modern British witchcraft and magic, the idea was not to 'think' morality as a guiding principle in the shaman's encounters with the beings of the otherworld, but rather to assess the usefulness of a familiar spirit (Wilby, 2005: 225). The question is thus not one of doubting the moral disposition of a spirit vis-à-vis the moral concerns of the shaman, but one of figuring out what works. In magic, it is action that leads the narrative forth, not moral concerns.

As to our own thoughts as magicians, shamans, card readers, or some other spiritual *cum* material workers, how 'good' or how 'bad' these thoughts may be, and what intent we have and what we want to use it for, I'd have to say this: The only obligation we have is not to speak and think good or bad of others, or speak and think good or bad of the earth and animals – on whose behalf we are also ever so ready to speak, often without calling. Rather, our obligation is to figure out how we can speak for ourselves first. And what does that mean? That means that we must know how to respect ourselves as the magicians who are capable of taking responsibility for the whole world if need be.

It is my belief that if we can respect ourselves as such, we can also respect others on whose behalf we may want to act. We can only expect of ourselves to do the 'right' thing if we know what it means to own up to our magical practice. This practice often starts with creating a space for the otherworld to inhabit. Who do we encounter there, and what kind of listening do we offer the ones who are willing to become our familiars? Do we question their morals in relation to our system of values, or do we go along with listening to what they propose? The only task we have in this relation is to assess to what extent what is being proposed is useful to what we want to accomplish, for indeed, this type of encounter does not mean having to give up our common sense. Hence the idea of negotiation in magic, making pacts, and honoring the mutual demands that arise.

In magic the law of similitude and correspondence only functions if action follows the intent. The more elaborate the action, the more it stresses the gravity of the intent. As a general rule we only need to go to the classical fairytales to get a sense of how the hero knows what the right thing to do is.

For instance, it is ever so clear what kind of forces the hero has to deal with, if we look at how these forces approach the person. If from behind, the hero can get ready to apply the lesson that the witch in the woods gave him before he set out to rescue the damsel in distress, which can be summed up as follows: 'Never turn back to face whatever approaches you from behind. Ask first why you're approached from behind, without turning to face this force. Then make your negotiations from the position you're in. Don't even think about moving, turning around, or running.' Such examples often make us think about what precisely is at stake when we realize that while we actually do know the difference between good and evil – we hardly need any moral philosophers to come along and preach it to us – we are less concerned with this distinction when we tell ourselves that what we want to achieve is results not evaluations of diverse moral dispositions.

Another example of how the idea of usefulness above morality is encoded into our actions, disclosing the ultimate unimportance of just how white or black the magic we're about to perform is, comes from folk magic. But before I go on, let me make it clear that my aim with these examples is not to endorse malefic acts, or belittle the benefic ones, but rather to show how magic is more about usefulness than about passing judgment. As I'm more familiar with the Romanian context, growing up with it, let me offer an instance of a spell from our magical popular consciousness that demonstrates how the magical deed, or what we call 'facatura' – from the Latin 'facere', to 'do' precisely, also similar to the 'fact' as conscious act – is related to a cause or consequence that is irreversible. Whereas white magic can be said to follow the rule of 'what is bound can also be unbound', black magic aims at irrevocability.

The point here is that one of the first things that a magician learns is to know the difference between the two. Why engage in either the one or the other, or why refuse to engage in the other for another, is a matter of detail, and has little to do with what we judge is either good or bad. But if we guide ourselves according to tested grimoirs and folk magic traditions, we realize, actually, how much dualism, or the difference between good and evil, is part of the ways in which we devise strategies for incorporating the one into the other. The fact that we may say 'no' to performing so-called 'dubious acts' is not a testimony of what magic is, and how colorful, but rather, it is a testimony of what we are, and how colorful.

Related to the casting of the evil eye, touched upon in the previous chapter, in the following example we have a narrative that stresses the conscious casting of a malefic spell. Note the elaborate steps of going about it, which suggests the gravity of the 'deed'. This example comes from a comparative study of folkloric magico-medical practices by I.A. Candrea (1944). I translate from the Romanian freely:

> If a woman wants to cast a spell of sickness unto another woman who behaved in a spiteful and malicious way towards her, she must do the following: For seven weeks every Sunday, at the time of high mass when the church bells are ringing, she must gather seven types of seeds from any plant and seven different berries. While collecting them, she must enchant them by stating her evil intent and the name of the person this deed is addressed to. Then she must put them into a little sack, sealing it with her song. After she's done, she must boil the contents of her sack in a pot that is stolen, and in water that is also collected

during the seven Sundays, or in untouched water every Sunday morning. Once the concoction is done, she must either pour it herself or send someone else to pour it on the threshold of the person she wants to harm, or on her way out of her house or work, or other path that the person takes regularly. The one who will first step on the concoction will be filled with the conjured sickness, but if the one it is intended for happens to step on it, then, behold, she will be in great danger and peril. (Candrea, 1944: 177)

What this passage tells us is that it requires a lot of dedication to perform black magic, suggesting indirectly that it is the fewest who will have either the patience to go through all of it, or the inclination. While the possibility is there, and one can also just hire a hit man for it if the idea of staying 'clean' is entertained, the point of the elaborate scheme is to discourage evildoers from engaging in casting malefic spells merely due to disagreements, no matter how serious these may be, or, at least give them time to think about it. It may well be that by the end of the seven Sundays, what may have seemed so urgent to do, no longer applies.

Now, while we may question such acts altogether, and hence refrain from having anything to do with harming another intentionally, magic in and of itself cares little about what we make of it. The best way to go about it is to keep the narratives apart, and rather than pass judgment on what other magicians do, and in the process praise ourselves for our taking the high road, we can simply try to pay attention to how we can serve the law of symmetry and balance.

The value of all magic is in its doing, not in our deeming it right or wrong. The primary presupposition here is that, insofar as the magician works under guidance once the threshold to the otherworld is crossed, she will be acting in accordance with her ability to not only negotiate her position in the otherworld, but also at the same time to renounce controlling what is to come out of it.

Given this frame I'm interested in magical acts that bypass the idea that we must have an ethical or moral code devised in our own image, or in that of some invented or proven tradition. A magical act is a magical act. Now, without continuing talking about magic as magic, as it is devoid of mainstream 'real' world regulations and hierarchies, I want to turn to talking about tools that make a statement on the applicability of magical acts in general. For this, I'll arm myself with the cards again, to give an example.

Basically I want to demonstrate how the Tarot can speak any language we want it to speak, by showing how neatly the cards can become part of a magical discourse performing on two levels: First as a divination tool – answering a question – and then as a tool for intervention, enforcing whatever acts that may have to do with the 'eating of the enemy', or the casting of benefic or malefic spells unto another. In the shamanic world, for instance, in addition to the common practice of casting, throwing concoctions or magical artifacts at another, or burying the other with view to disarming them, the magician can also perform the eating of a talisman or an amulet as a sign of complete annihilation or, indeed, as the case may also be, as a representation and performance of a healing.

ACT AND BELIEF

For this I have decided to pose a double-edged question, or a question that addresses not only a specific topic, but also how this topic can be seen to answer back beyond the interpretative level. What I'm interested in is to establish a contrast between act and belief with view to investigating to what extent we may dissociate act from belief in our magical practice. In other words, the underlying question to the question proper is whether it even makes any sense to muddle the levels and introduce belief, an abstract entity, into a concrete act, which magic requires. For instance, does my belief or lack thereof in the use of magical puppets, knives, pins, and the like, add anything of value to the act itself of stabbing with view to inflicting harm on another? The same applies to an act of blessing. My theory is that while faith is required, as everything in the magical realm is given to us in grace, our own beliefs contribute little to how magic actually works. But let us have a concrete look at how the cards may help us understand what is at stake here. For this question I use a classical 13-card spread, or what I like to call 'the council of 13':

> *How practical are magical acts and how do they serve*
> *the practitioner beyond his or her beliefs in good and evil?*

I read first the inner cross, then the outer cross, then the diagonal lines in the main square of 9 cards, and then the themes around the inner cross cards[1]. I will first read for the magical interpretation, and then look at what the cards may spell out if this was a reading for a mundane issue. The idea is to keep in mind the possibility of the cards to function as an oracle and as a talisman. The latter will be particulary explored in the chapters to come.

––––––––

1 For an in-depth introduction to the mechanics of reading this spread, see my book, *Marseille Tarot: Towards the Art of Reading.*

CHEVALIER DE BATON.

LE IUGEMENT.

VALET DE BATON.

XVIII

LE SOLEIL.

VII

LE CHARIOT.

VALET DES COUPES

III

ROY DE DENIER

XII

LE PENDU.

THE MAGICAL READING

As we can see from the beginning, the practicability of magic is found in the desire to change our emotional content. As most magical acts are the result of emotion, ranging from rage to bliss, the 9 of Cups here reflects that need very accurately and neatly. So we read around this card of change the following:

If you put energy (The Sun) into your magical intent, you'll succeed (The Charioteer). But as we can see here by looking at the Charioteer, we also get the distinct impression that while winning the stake, we must also take leave of it. In some magical discourses it is, in fact, an imperative that if you have just exercised your intent, or will, you must leave it to work.[2] You are not to check your bun in the oven every third minute to see if it grows. You must trust that it does, leave it at that, have faith, and then practice the art of patience.

The magic manifests in the world in the following way: First you ride your horse to the otherworld (Knight of Batons), and meet the gatekeeper (King of Coins) who is willing to listen to why you're there: Presumably because what you need is impossible to obtain in your ordinary reality (The Hanged Man, towards whom the King is turned, suggests that much). Other messengers support the brilliant force that goes into effecting change (Sun to Charioteer): The Pages of Batons and Cups, mirroring each other and flanking the action around the fountain, are both oriented towards the center of attention, where things are stirred in the 9 cups. The Page of Batons adds more logs to the fire while the Page of Cups pours some champagne onto the head of the winner. But the big cup of abundance (Ace of Cups) does not

---

2   See Doreen Valiente's works.

serve all equally well, as someone gets hanged (the Hanged Man). Has the Charioteer gone overboard with the libation? Going from the Ace of Cups straight to the 9 of Cups suggests a rapid, overflowing power that may drown the eager traveller. Has the traveller remembered to pay his dues to the gatekeeper? Is the King of Coins telling the Hanged Man that he needs to give up agency? Indeed, over in the otherworld one needs to renounce one's shining armor, and, as I've said before, place oneself at the mercy of the otherworldly powers.

The spirit world (Judgment) accepts the act of surrendering, announcing that the magician will be granted her wish (9 of Cups is the card of the heart's desire *par excellence*), and she will be allowed to act as an intermediary between spirit and the one she wishes to act on behalf of (3 of Cups).

The outer message is that some cuts are needed, but that these are not to be violent but subtle (4 of Swords to 2 of Swords). The King of Coins himself presides over the conflict, yet suggesting that since we are not here with any active swords that cut right through the core of the matter, separating the wheat from the chaff must allow for our assessing what we make of the mirroring of the above and the below. What do the swords above and the swords below tell us?

There is some preparation involved here, as we may consider this visual image: Instead of feeling that we are hemmed in at all 4 corners, we might consider the idea that we are in a room equipped with one sword on each wall. Whicever way we turn, we have the option of grabbing any of the 4 swords and go to meet our rival. In fact, as an act of courtesy, we might invite the other into the room, and hand him a sword too. With the two swords clenched, we don't hear the blades, but rather what is between them, perhaps a moment of beauty, the release of perfume, the promise of healing. 'As above, so below,' calls us here to listen.

If we look at the emerging themes here, we might say the following: There is a burning desire to hit home base (Ace of Cups, Page of Batons, 3 of Coins, around the Sun). A call is made, a cup is offered, and alternative options are considered (Judgment, Page of Cups, The Hanged Man, around The Charioteer).

The initial flowing zest dries up but there's some theatrical resurrection (Ace of Cups, 4 of Swords, Judgment, around the Knight of Batons). The incubated magical act requires constraint and a renunciation (3 of Coins, 2 of Swords, The Hanged Man, around the King of Coins).

In other words, magical acts work and they serve the practitioner well, insofar as the practitioner is ready to sacrifice something too: travel to the otherworld and surrender to what happens there. Messages may be concretely symmetrical, enticing the magician to an active attitude or a passive reflection, but they may also be indirect. Making an offering of libation or money is also part of the deal. Perhaps donning a costume and carriage of power helps, and arriving at the scene dancing in the public limelight might give the spirits something to laugh at. But at the end of the day, one must show willingness to be stripped of one's control in exchange for a magical solution.

Generally in a magical reading there's the tendency to look at what the swords are doing, as they are associated with the magical craft. Given also the preamble I've made here to begin with, by referring to all things black magic, stabbing and stirring the pot with iron, I could say that the practicality of a magical act consists of fixing the blind spots. The swords here in mirroring position – indeed, as above, so below – suggest that the way to magic comes at a price. As you make your cuts in accordance, you participate in establishing poetic justice. In this sense, magic is not a question of working AT but working WITH. We may need structuralist rules that get us there, over the threshold; we may even need to insist on the dualism of good and evil, such as we may find it in the type of sacred magic developed by Western hermetic esotericism, where the renunciation of our desire below results in reward above, but the thing is that once we're there – call it heaven or hell – other('s) rules apply. 'There' you work WITH, which means that there is no-self to worry about. There is no morality. This is the lesson of the Hanged Man.

However, when I'm saying this, I don't mean to suggest that magic is amoral. What I am saying is that what makes a world magical is not what we claim it is, but what we experience it is beyond our distinctions of dualism. Insofar as the magician is with one foot in the world of logos and the other in the world of mythos, the only task she has, if she is to succeed, is to watch her step. Which is not the same as saying that she must act out of a 'moral' intent to begin with, or presume that through her own effort she will achieve anything worth the while. I think that a true magician operates from within a space of grace. And this has very little to do with what we make of it culturally speaking.

In the magical context the cards above suggest that all magic operates with the usefulness of our actions against the background of our giving up entirely all other systems of belief that we may have inherited or built ourselves, be they moral, ethical, or otherwise. The fact that the whole reading gravitates towards the Hanged Man, the last card down in this layout, spells out the necessity to do magic from within a complete change of heart, a change that has renunciation at the core, and the willingess to see things from a perspective that places our heads down, that leaves one of our legs in suspension and the other tied to what links us to where we have come from.

Given the question, the above reading is clearly more descriptive than interventional. Here, the card reader must always remember what the inital task is, what room she operates within, and for what purpose. It is not a good idea to start out with a divinatory aim, and then, half the way through it, decide that the cards must now be used as talismans, or some other thing that supports active intervening with one's own business or that of another. Some card readers advocating for the so-called intuitive readings may argue that if the cards decide to take you to another magical room than the divinatory gypsy tent, then you must obey and go along. I don't want to contradict this position. But I do want to say that I don't find such shifting of the mind conducive to any concrete solution that one is after. I find that whenever the mixing of the levels of action happens, a loss of focus also happens. Clarity and coherence disappear, and what is left are just claims without any commonsensical basis.

A magical performance is only practical as long as we are willing to go along with our suspension of disbelief, and then in this suspension find that we no longer need whatever our cultures dictate. What we need is to see that, as magicians, we can walk the tighrope upside down, and realize that we are never falling. But before we get there, we must be able to recognize the path we're walking, and if we got it wrong, we must take responsibility for it, rather than indulge in exclaiming to ourselves in surprise, to cover up for the loss of face: 'What a delightfully foolish enterprise this particular journey was.' A magician with respect for herself will demonstrate robustness of character, whenever her mind will fail to make the proper distinctions. Magic begins in the mind, not in our gut feeling, emotions, or some other intuitive anatomical or psychic prompters. We would do well to remember that without the brain power that we bring to our actions, there would be no emotional charging of anything: No moving of the mountains, and no riding on the broom. No conjuring of winds, and no guiding of the souls to their resting place. No reading of cards that resonates, and no symbolic actions with efficient intent.

THE MUNDANE READING

Now, if I wasn't reading this spread for a specific magical purpose, or even for a meta-question as above – a question of practicality about practicality – but rather, to know something about the magic of the banal in the everyday life that goes through three known stages – you get born, you live, you die – I'd probably say the following:

Two get together to form a family. The economics of it is in the high seat (Ace of Cups, The Sun, 3 of Coins). The family is already large with children of all ages and coming from all corners of the world (the 2 Pages, The Knight of Batons). The smaller kids are close to the family (the pages are doing similar things on the same plane), while the older one (the knight) is trying to impress his father. Yet he comes from a position that's informed by a destabilizing attitude (4 of Swords). The father (King of Coins) is not convinced, as he feels separated from his son (2 of Swords). The family is good at keeping up the appearances and making a lot of noise (Judgment), while also displaying a virile driving force (Charioteer). In reality, however, this pushing forward ends with incapacity, as all is out to hang (the Hanged Man).

There was great love in the past (Ace of Cups, The Sun), but right now it is strained and about to change (9 of cups). This is due to too many destabilizing factors (the Swords are strategically placed, suggesting that what is in the head and what is walked on is painful). The general visual imagery supports this reading: We can see how the two people in the Sun card become two horses in the Charioteer card. The shining sun itself turns into a shining armor, adorning more of a costume than a man in control of his horses. Judging by the position of the Hanged Man, we can see that this driver has little knowledge of what he is doing, ending his ride in a ditch. Similarly, while the crowd that includes the extended family (Judgment) still cheers for the maintenance of the status quo (The Charioteer), the man in the house grows impotent (the Hanged Man). As they say, however, worse things can happen.

The outer cards are all masculine, and except for the Page of Cups, we're dealing here with fast cards. For me, the batons are faster than the swords. When the batons are in the air, they work with the wind. When the swords are in the air, they work with the skills of whoever holds them. And last I've checked, man has never been faster than the wind. Also, the batons in the earth grow faster than the iron, or minerals that go into a sword. So we can conclude that the reason why this spread ends with a sense of regret, is due to the fact that there's little pondering here. Too much malicious action and very little thinking about it (no active swords indicating at least a full-blown honest war; only the same old conflict, as the 4 of Swords participates in stabilizing and maintaining the general tension indicated by the 2 of Swords).

Moreover, from this mundane perspective the absence of women may be worrying. The only glimpse we get of a woman is in the Sun card. But there she is on the same level as the other, having exactly as much agency as the other. In and of itself, the idea of sharing everything on a mutual basis is a beautiful thing, but if this sharing becomes a whole circus run by male power, then things are not so good anymore.

Now, while this reading clearly has a level of concreteness that may appeal to many, the question to ask is the following: Couldn't this reading also apply to the magical context? Indeed it could, only, as we have our eye precisely on the way in which our question is formulated, we must adapt our nuances in our interpretations to the specific context of the question. For instance, I could say that the supposed gatekeeper in the magical reading, namely, the King of Coins, is not a father figure, but rather a collector of souls: In goes a coin, and out pops a breath. As soon as the magician gets to the otherworld, he expiates. But here then, it would be interesting to ask, why? Why does the Charioteer experience a loss of control with the consequence of hanging? Is it because once he's in the otherworld he no longer needs the same means of transport that got him there to begin with? This is very likely.

As card readers when must constantly proceed from what the narrative presents us with as we go along, and we must look at what new twists in the narrative we experience that are consistent with the framing of our question. We must seek to address what is likely and what is plausible. After all, in a reading with the cards we are not after depicting fairytales and unicorns, unless, of course, that is the aim to begin with. Without a clearly formulated question, there is no coherent interpretation. The interpretation that deviates from the context of the question is no longer an interpretation, but rather the invention of fiction.

FREE FALL MAGIC

Because I value magic for offering us the possibility to step outside of ourselves, yet at the same time keep a vigilant eye on our intent and where it gets us, I prefer to see that it stays magical. We do not need to impose any rules on magic, least of all contaminate it with our talk about what is right and what is wrong.

Magic, like divination, relies on a system. If we don't have a method, we are not likely to be able to jump at experiencing anything magical. Only frustration. Magic is not mysticism, in the sense of the latter manifesting by surprise. Magical consciousness is very much the result of what we expect. So the form of our expectation, namely that specific magic happens, influences the content. If we expect to see monsters, we'll be likely to see monsters. But while magic is not as surprising as a mystical experience – where the mystical stands for the spiritual meaning that is not apparent to either our senses or capacity to reason – magic can just happen in the sense that it makes us realize that our senses and intelligent capacity are enhanced beyond awe.

In magical time we act, in mystical time we don't. In magical time, if we see a monster or an angel we are not merely 'struck' by the vision, and expectant to hear a message beyond the unintelligible. If we don't like what we see, we don't necessarily stop there, at making an aestehtic evaluation: 'I don't think I like this'. Rather, we may easily end up having a nice conversation, or a frightening one, with the beings or sensations we encounter. We say 'hello' and 'goodbye', ask concrete questions, negotiate, make offerings and promises. We may decide on the spot that the particular monster we've encountered must be either vanquished or befriended. So we snap our two fingers, and abracadabra, our conversational partner either disappears, or ends up telling us a secret. We then come back from the land of 'woo' with a clear sense of accomplishment. We feel like a genuine hero in a fairytale: We did it.

Influential occultist Lon Milo Duquette has a simple way of articulating what is happening in magical time: 'It's all in your head... you just have no idea how big your head is' (subtitle on the cover of *Low Magick*). In this sense the art of magic is a simple art. First you have to trick your mind to get over the threshold, and then, once there, you have to let yourself be at the mercy of the rules applying there. In principle, you also very rarely need any artificial ritual or costume. If you do don a costume, it will be for the sake of honoring the dead, animal spirit, or the spectating witnesses, who expect to see something that exceeds their ordinary reality. This theatricality may help them to get out of their own heads and concerns.

The art or magic becomes grace when you see whatever you have in your head manifest in the world. Magic is thus for 'doing' not just for 'trying'. We pay attention to symmetries, to what's above and below us, and to how this attends to the way in which our will reflects our passions and feelings in order to experience an expansion of our consciousness. In this sense, it is hard to see how we can think 'morals', or where exactly we can fit morality into the process of rationalizing our gut instincts. If we want magic, we can simply start with asking for permission to enter a world whose doors open with a deck of cards, or a drum, or a mask. 'Open Sesame' is only as powerful as we make it. This is not a power phrase for political correctness, but rather an invitation to not let our cultural concerns initiate our experiences. Magic happens when the mystery of action takes hold of control.

NATURAL MAGIC
FOUR RITUALS AND A SOUL

Be still, and know that I am God.
– Psalm 46: 10

Having gone thus far through a few ideas about principles of magic with cards based on my personal experience and ensuing storytelling about these experiences, I now want to move into an area that concretely spells out how we can work magically with the cards in the best possible way, so that we get a sense of greater connection to our fellow humans, animals, and nature.

What connects our cognitive capacity with the observations about the world and our place in it? Can we feel this connection at the level of the body, the intelligence of our gut, and the power to surrender to experiencing the world through grace rather than personal effort? Can we distinguish between what we call personal, spiritual development and our capacity to be present in the world for the sake of others? Why do we seek guidance? What do we do with the insights we get? Keep them or share them?

These are some of the questions that I will attempt to answer first by going through a natural magic cycle, and then considering what we call 'soulwork' in the context of a philosophy of action.

SEASONING THE TEMPERAMENT

What follows is basically one main ritual of natural magic in five parts that I have recently devised for one of my students of magic and the sacred arts. I am thoroughly grateful to Elizabeth Owen for allowing me to use her example in its entirety. Without the generosity of the people seeking a connection with the sacred arts, there would be no magic around.

The style of the following rituals is direct address, enticing the student to action and feedback. In order for the reader to be able to follow this process of working with people on a one-to-one basis, I have kept the format (content, order, and time) of these rituals in which I have delivered them.

For the purpose of this book, I have, however, deliberately left out an entire reading of a natal chart according to Renaissance astrology methods, but it is relevant to mention that the ritual was anchored in directing the elemental magic around the telluric forces. In reading this chart, it was clear that what was lacking, and hence needed, was a firm focus on the element of earth.

As my attention was primarily given to four main relations in the chart, namely the Ascendant, the Giver of Life (hyleg), the Lord of Geniture (the strongest planet that can act), the moon phase, and overall temperament, the first initial magical act was an introduction to the element that was absent, in this case here, the earth, seen from the perspective of what the planets related to the four relations had to say about it in synthesis.

The main driving force was to have the earth kiss the student hello, as it were, and hence let that kiss permeate the subsequent rituals devised around the four classical elemental powers: earth, water, air, and fire. In other words, the telluric force was set to drive the cartomantic narrative forward, independently of where the individual focus lay otherwise, that is to say, on each of the four elements that we shall meet shortly. As each ritual was anchord in a divination with the cards, the reading of the cards unfolded against the background of the knowledge that an enhanced awareness of the earth needed to be present in all the actions.

The choice for the telluric force as an introduction to the four rituals was primarily given through an analysis of the student's temperament, which I have established as phlegmatic[1], that is, of moist and cold orientation.

Generally, the phlegmatic is characterized by strong desires. Very strong. The trouble with the phlegmatic type, however, is that going for strong feelings does not always mean going for strong, good feelings. Also, desiring to feel desire itself is connected to not having any boundaries to feeling. This amounts to having a desire to go out to feel something, but not actually going through with it, as the phlegmatic often finds it a pain to actually have to leave the house and do it.

In other words, the phlegmatic likes the idea of feeling even more than she likes the emotion itself, as this emotion is never defined concretely from the point of view of desire. The consequence is that the phlegmatic can easily find herself desiring ecstatic experience even when this feeling does not take any particular shape.

Consequently, the whole point of having an introduction to the rituals anchored in what needs attention – here, how to ground desire – is to address the blind spot in failing to recognize

---

1   For the assessment of temperament I have used John Frawley's variables and techniques from his book: *The Real Astrology Applied* (2002).

just how one can situate oneself vis-à-vis one's desires as they unfold themselves against the background of a platform for action that one actually has available to oneself beyond the desiring point.

The following introductory ritual is thus based on bringing awareness to the cold and moist aspects of the earth (as the case was here). For this I have not used the visual common sense suggested by the cards, but rather a simple, natural approach, in the form of command.

TELLURIC FORCES ACTION

Go out in nature. Find a tree to sit by. Make sure that there are some flowers growing about whose roots are bulbs. They contain water. You need to get to the truth of the earth as filtered through water. The earth will channel its power towards you through this medium.

Dig a small hole around the plant, and try to feel its bulb. Squeeze it gently, without suffocating it. Ask for permission first.

Make the following invocation:

Reveal thy truth to me, oh, earth, reveal thy truth.
Ashes to ashes, rain on the ashes.

Take your hands out, and shake them. The warmth of your body will create some condensed moisture.

Take some earth into both your palms. Close your palms. Sit by the tree and acknowledge its roots. You are welcome to intellectualize what you're doing.

Ask yourself: 'Why am I doing this?'
Let your left hand answer.
Ask yourself: 'What is this teaching?'
Let your right hand answer.

Call on Venus, ruler of earth and money, and Lord of Geniture,
your strongest ally according to your natal astrological chart.
Ask Venus: 'What is beyond desiring desire?'
Let your throat answer.

Call on the Moon, ruler of water and hearth.
Ask the Moon to grant you the desire for earth.

Say thank you to all.

Close the ritual by drawing on the earth the sign of the earth,
the circle with the quadrant houses. Place your finger in the middle of it. Then kiss your finger. Allow yourself to taste the earth.

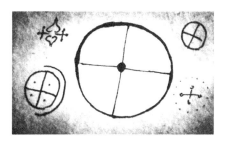

You're welcome to write to me about this experience, but try
to keep to the essentials of it. Do these essentials address the
aim of this first ritual? In what way? How do you feel you're ready
(or not) for the next step, which is a more focused encounter with
the elements through the power of the earth? Keep going.

EARTH RITUAL

It is so that when one engages on the magical path, the first realization is that nothing is made, but all is given. What do I mean by this in concrete terms? How does it relate to the overall aim of letting the telluric forces manifest through us, so that we become better at integrating the elemental forces of nature into our lives? Just think. Today is the New Moon.

As I write these very words down, the new moon culminates exactly into my living room. I'm writing this for you on the new moon. The new moon is for beginnings. I find this very appropriate in the context of our common aim here, for me to teach you something, and for you to experience it as magic.

But what do we call this coincidence? Did I plan for this ritual for you to do it on the new moon, this lovely April night? Indeed, I had done no such thing. So what can we call it then? I call it 'the given'. From my perspective, if I get to devise this special ritual for you in accordance with my own magical intent, I do it by the grace of god. You can choose to name this 'grace' or this 'god' anything you like, but for me it is a clear indication that we are not anymore with what we create ourselves in terms of planning, or what we make of it, the situation, that is, but rather, it is about realizing just how magic works.

Thus, I look at your cards for this earth ritual, based on this concrete question:

What do you need to start with, so that you can get the telluric forces flow through you, and so that you can see a concrete manifestation of these forces as they spell out 'earth' on your body?

The Tower, The Moon, Temperance

In case we should still entertain some expectations, I'd say that with these cards we are not disappointed. But we must push forward, and beyond that, beyond having to say, 'wow, this exceeds what I'm thinking, what I've been expecting.' What we want is to not *think,* but to *live* magic in action. Thinking will be integrated into that action, so it becomes redundant in the larger scheme.

The oracle speaks:

All that is man-made must go. It must simply fall down. All that you have learnt and built for yourself must be smashed, where magic is concerned. You do not approach magic from any tower, whether of wisdom, constraint, or any other such constructions. Magic is not the thing of our hands, or our thoughts, of our capacity to discern. Magic is raw power.

You must go out into the wild. Not too far from the city, though. The card of the Moon guides you to a place by a pond.

There, at night, under the moonbeams, you can allow yourself to contemplate the towers of civilization, but you will have crossed the hedge already into making new realizations.

You must learn to know your place in this world, and one way of doing that is by looking at ways of integrating what you are with the earth you're standing on, and what you aspire to become, one with the same earth you're standing on. There must be balance.

One of the most magnificent earth wisdoms that we have passed down to us is formulated in the saying that the ideal is to walk in beauty and balance. The card of Temperance enforces that here.

The way of magic makes itself known in these first three cards very clearly: You encounter the earth outside of the place of dwellings, where you can allow yourself to smell your own fears. But someone will watch over you. Spirit, nature itself, will know why you are there, why you have come.

Based on this divination, and what the cards suggest, here is a simple earth ritual:

ACTION

Take a black candle to symbolize the tower that now reverts to the earth. What is man-made must go back to nature, melt down into the earth. Let the light of the candle symbolize this new awareness that everything is earth and to earth everything returns.

Go to a place in nature at night, and sit by a pond or water. You may want to find this place during daylight first.

Once you spot where you want to sit, tell the place of your intention, namely, that you want to come there by night, to sit there for a while, in the moon light. Try to do this when the moon is waxing.

To honor the power of the moon, and what it can teach you about the earth, have a black obsidian surface with you – if you have an obsidian mirror it would be perfect. If not, find a small container – cast iron is great for this – fill it with water, and throw a silver coin into it.

As you gaze into the blackness and past the coin, ask the moon to reflect into the silver mirror what you are and what you aspire to.

Ask the moon to help you integrate into your earthly being what you have inherited.

Ask the moon to help you integrate into your earthly desires what you aspire to become.

Place a strong emphasis on your being as earth that breathes and is alive.

Have some libation with you in the form of milk. When you are done, sprinkle the contents of your container over the place where you sat. Offer your thanks to the earth, and thank the moon for its messages.

Write down whatever you feel inspired to share with me, or whatever you would like to keep to yourself.

Blessings of the New Moon.

May it bring you an awareness of how your being is aligned with the pulse of the earth, and how this pulse can teach you to walk in beauty and balance.

Keep going.

WATER RITUAL

For the water ritual, I have formulated this question, while thinking of science and statistics, and how everyone seems to agree that not only do our bodies consist mostly of water, but they are also profoundly influenced by it. So my question was under the influence of some depth:

What do you need to do to get in touch with water, feel its force, and use it as magic?

The Pope, Judgment, The Devil

As often in my work with the cards, I am ever so grateful for the very concrete answers they give me. These answers teach me as much as they teach you, and I'm always pleasantly surprised to see how the cards address headlong just what is needed. This one here was quite easy, as the way the cards fell on the table was aligned very much with what I was thinking.

More immediately we're here in the presence of this concrete piece of advice: What you need is a self-baptism; a baptism that takes care of your lower body, rather than your head. If you've ever participated in a Catholic baptism, you will have seen how the priest, or the pope himself, pours water on the baby's head. Your cards suggest that you do that to your nether regions. The Devil is the master of the underworld, so anything that has to do with the lower part of everything will be his domain. Here, I was thinking of how important our fluids are, and how we often don't pay much attention to them, especially when they relate to the part of the body that makes secretions from the genitals. But we're not here with the world of shame and cultural constructs, so here is what I suggest.

These cards indicate that you will simply get to know water if you allow yourself to baptize your own vagina.

ACTION

Take a chalice that's reminiscent of the baptismal font that you find in old cathedrals. If you can find one made from marble it would be great. Why marble? Because the card of Judgment suggests it. People come out of some marble tombs, so there seems to be some earth power connected to the whiteness of marble, alluding also to the silver moon, the mother of all creation. Without the moon there would be no ebbing and flowing, and probably no life at all. White marble also alludes to purification and strength. Water can blend with the solidity of marble highlighting the gravity of what you're doing.

Take this chalice and fill it with running water. You may want to get it from your friend, the pond you were sitting by for the previous ritual.

Stand over it, and start splashing yourself with this water in a movement that allows you to get it inside you. Don't be afraid to use your hands.

Then say the following or something similar (these are my own words, but you can find yours if you prefer):

I am water, the earth is water. We are bound.

I baptize the source of creation, my source.

I baptize my source.

Water, come and wash my dreams.

The moon beams.

Then go to bed and ask water to give you a sign. Before falling asleep, make sure you induce yourself into an incubatory state. That is, make sure you maintain this thought, that you want water to teach you its lesson, so that you know water. You can do this for several nights in a row. Place a bowl of water by your bed too, and ask water to take away all that which interferes with the passing of beneficial messages on to you through your dreams.

Blessings of the water.
Keep going.

AIR RITUAL

As I'm writing these words, while suffering from high fever and gasping for air – the price for going to too many conferences – I am thinking about the tasks we must perform when our 'powers' may be limited. But then I realized that Air, calling on Air to clear myself first, and then calling on it to show you how you can use its power, is quite appropriate for this state. When we burn up, for whatever reason, a cool breeze is all we need. But then we must also learn to control the potential major blowing that makes our blaze burn everything up.

Air is a very good friend to have, like all the other elements, but once we engage on this path, we will slowly realize who of the four is our strongest ally. Air works for me in wondrous way. It cleanses me, it tells me things, and it makes me listen to the wind's whisper. We understand the elements through something other than our conscious minds.

Just as we talk about embodiment, when we look at the Tarot cards and try to figure out which function each card fulfills, so it is with the elements. If we can embody them, we are each and every one of them. We are the elements already, of course, but the way we constantly forget that forces us to think consciously of how we can recuperate what is lost in our amnesia. Perhaps it is in the very act of recuperation that we get to sense what kind of magic we are capable of, for indeed, any magic requires focalization. Not representation, but presence. By this I mean that every act of magic requires the recognition of a system of correspondences – or inventing one, if it doesn't exist – so that we can bring ourselves to the site of what we can understand experientially.

With this in mind, thinking of the way Air enables us to think of ourselves as birds, flying through freedom and feeling the wind in our hairs, I have asked the cards on your behalf the following:

How can I know Air?
What must I be aware of in order to feel the force of Air, also as it relates to a basic form of grounding?

The Star, The Empress, Judgment

As usual, you get the cards that you need. Quite appropriate here, as there's little to say, other than:

ACTION

Get naked again one starry night, arm yourself with water as your ally, and start offering your libation to the earth.

You are the Empress. You can say out loud what you came to ask for. Let the stars shine on you, while you ask Air to caress your body and teach you its lessons. In other Marseille Tarots, such as the Tarot of Jean Dodal (1701), the card of the Star features a bird in the tree behind the woman. We don't have one here, but we can imagine it nearby. The card of the Empress already testifies to the fact that you can imagine it, as we find here a bird on her shield, the emblem of her achievements.

Indeed, as I seem to have anticipated it, you can know Air by creating a system of correspondence. The bird that flies free can be captured by your imagination and used as a talisman.

Whenever you need to call on Air, you call the bird. Craft a coin that features a bird on it. I can let you in on a secret. Magi of old used to invoke the fixed star Spica, one of the most benefic stars there is. They used to make talismans with Spica's sigil and her emblem on them. This emblem is a bird.

The last thing that you then need is to simply sharpen your ears. When the Angel blows his trumpet, a lot of air comes out of it. But it's the kind of air that has meaning attached to it. Go out in public and try to penetrate what Air tells you.

In esoteric circles, one speaks of the language of the birds, as the language that opens up our doors of perception. Many think that vowels are the most magical letters because they are full of wind. Invoke the Air by using vowels, and listen:

Air cool and Air hot: A E I O U
Walk the wind in lavish trot: I A I A O H

With flying blessings, IAO.
Keep going.

FIRE RITUAL

According to the Romanian folklore, after the summer solstice on June 21st, the gates to heaven are open for three more days. Particularly the night between the 23rd and 24th is significant, as that is the night when the fairies descend to the earth, or when they can be spotted through the veil separating the visible from the invisible world.

The Romanians celebrate this night by making great bonfires, yet not in the usual way of piling up the wood logs and letting them burn high to the sky, but rather, by making wheel-shaped wreaths, the size of human bodies, and pouring resin oil between the braids. These are then taken up to the top of the hills around the village, and with the fire in them, young boys let them roll down. The fire makes a counter clockwise movement to the movement of the wheel itself, suggesting burning all that which runs counter to our lives and is not useful. This night is called the Night of the Faeries, or in Romanian, *Noaptea Sanzienelor.*

This night is all about the power of fire, and what fire can do. Fire is not the thing that contemplates. Fire burns and blasts. Fire purifies and cleanses. According to the Romanian tradition, after the wheel of fire rolls down and vanishes to ashes, young girls and women take over. They pray to the Sanziene for their power of fertility, healing, and good luck, and then they collect the early morning dew to bathe in.

I particularly like the involvement of the elderflower for a sacred bath, and after that, enjoying some homemade, pearly elderflower lemonade, while letting the steam in the body cool down. It's enough to keep a woman very happy after having just burnt a lot of the unnecessary load we all carry around the whole year.

For your fire ritual, and as ever, I have asked the cards the same question, with a slight variation:

How can you know fire?

What can you do to know its purifying power without getting burnt yourself?

How can you know the benefic intensity of fire without having to blow exhaustingly into it to keep it?

As ever, and again to my pleasant surprise, the cards describe the situation quite to the point. I have to say that I often think that the way in which the cards allow me to create rituals for myself and others is simply the best. It's as if the cards not only enforce my belief in the blessings and wisdom we can receive from reading them, but they also insist on showing me exactly that which puts all my doubts to rest. The fact also that they don't just tell me things about myself, but also suggest ways of being in the world through more considerate connections, fires all my passions.

While shuffling the cards, I started out with thinking about the Romanian fire wreaths and how I might say something about the tradition I grew up with so that I honor it, when I realized that the cards had decided that, indeed, you must also see what I'm thinking of. You must also be part of my ancestral connections.

The World, The Tower, The Emperor

There you have it. Here we get the wreath, the blasting tower coming down as a consequence of fire, and the gathering of the self in the form of taking imperial control over the situation, or at least acknowledging the fact that the fire has fixed that which we often can't bring ourselves to fix, and that we can learn from it.

Perhaps we could say that you can know fire by its circling power. Without a circle of fire around us, we would not know passion. Without fire from above, fire that is beyond our cultural grasp, we cannot know about its surprising dimension – for better or worse. We may start the fire; we may consciously put fire into our wreaths and weaves, and then, when we're done with our prayers, we may feed the fire our magical work. But once the fire takes hold of us and our possessions, we must know that either we learn how to control it, or all is lost.

The cards here complete this very circle that goes back to the first ritual for the earth power. Ashes to ashes, we say, and dust to dust. Indeed, when fire is done with its dance, all goes back into the belly of the earth. When gravity calls, there's no ash that goes somewhere else than inside the earth. No ash, the imprint of fire, can hide.

The Emperor here tells us the following: Controlling the fire is power – power also over declaring that when the rite is over and the world shifts once again, we must all go back to work. 'Chop wood and carry water,' the Buddhists say, and they are right.

Perhaps this is the lesson of the fire that you must learn, or at least consider: When all is turned to ashes, you must stomp the ground with your feet, and be ready to build anew. The purifying fire is the force the builds and rebuilds; from character to coven. Fire touches all and burns all.

ACTION

To know fire, try the following:

- Make a round wreath from flowers and feathers, and sprinkle it with animal fat.
- Take it inside your house and offer it to the fire.
- Into the fire you may also throw puppets of people you're done with (hold the death wish, though).
- Take a scepter in your hand, or a wooden wand, and contemplate the burning.
- Resolve to rise again purified and clean, and with clear, controlling vision.
- Let the fire teach you the value of burning, and the value of returning the ashes to the earth.

May the power of the four elements be with you.
Keep going.

SOULWORK

A simple magical cycle such as the one suggested here makes us realize that wisdom comes as a result of paying attention to what we can do concretely for our souls. What acts can we perform and according to what rules? If these rules are not of our making, can we live with them? And how do we get our soul to align itself with the magic of the everyday life and our pragmatic concerns with what we are for ourselves and others?

I distinguish between two kinds of work: cards in your face and cards in your soul – the latter in the tradition of soulmaking à la William Blake and Walt Whitman, when we are interested in knowing whether the perception of a certain thought we entertain – joyful, or suicidal – is actually 'reality'. Regardless of which – and we have ways of determining just what we're dealing with, a pragmatic or an abstract situation – the bottom line for me is this one: whatever you do or think, project or speculate, make sure you don't insult your soul, as Whitman proclaimed. If there's anything that puts me off, then it's the situation that I identify as being devoid of basic respect and self-respect. So, indeed, whatever you do, don't insult your soul.

I identify soulwork with the work of realizing that what society wants you to do is not the same as what your soul wants you to do. And why? Because society is self-interested. The soul is not. Society will do anything to convince you that working for it is something that you absolutely love, and that, consequently, it is also good for your soul. This is the kind of nonsense that only makes sense if we consider the idea that image is everything. Indeed it is, from the vantage point of societal rules and constraints.

Imagine if we grew up with a different type of desire than the kind related to language; dictating differently: 'thy *shalt* covet your neighbor's possessions, his wife and his house, and everything else he's got.' The Bible instructs us in the dangers of this desire, but we do it anyway, yet won't admit it.

The soul has some other ways of accessing knowledge, and this knowledge is not always the so-called consecrated one: Here's a new diploma for you, well done, and congratulations. The soul has no agenda other than to put you in an ecstatic mode. You are, after all, going to die very soon, so why not be ecstatic in the meantime? So, soulwork is doing work that seeks to integrate an ecstatic mode – answering that call – with a societal call, one that tends to put a lid on your ecstasy. And why are we interested in soulWORK? Because not everyone is interested in retiring to a cave and becoming a mystical monk. The main question thus remains: How to do 'social' work without insulting your soul? How to say, 'yes sir', to your imbecile boss, without running out of his office with the desire to call him names and send the whole institution that he stands for straight to hell. You are insulted to your core. While that may feel like a good idea, the trouble is that there's nothing more deadening to a magician than taking offence, for that would mean that she lacks the capacity for detachment, which is one of the primary conditions for successful magic.

Where soulwork is concerned, I have to admit that I have a weakness for all nondualist philosophy. I like hanging out with nondualist philosophers, as they make you kiss a donkey, love it too, and then run naked in the fields. There's nothing that's inappropriate. There is just you and what you can imagine moves through you. I admit that I approach soulwork from that perspective of not worrying about how compassionate I am, how sympathetic I am with my own situation and that of others, how good I am at being non-judgmental, how loving I am, or how often I can say after every line, 'peace be with you'. I don't worry about any of that. I zoom in only on what my soul has to say vis-à-vis what embodies it, man and culture alike. You can't have compassion come from a place that you don't own, from dictations.

My own nondualist inclinations make me tend to integration – and this can be as physical or as metaphysical as I like it to be, such as, for instance, the situation when I walk into a classroom and have to make sure that what I teach is not only in accordance with the 'quality' rules devised in the curriculum, and the 'relevance' of my stuff, but also that this teaching does not run counter to what my soul abhors, which is institutional clichés.

As a checklist of how I'm doing in this department, namely balancing between what I need to give Caesar and what I need to give God, that is, my own soul, I invent rituals of sitting out in nature, or read cards and listen to their message. They always seem to have a view of the situation that's more authentic than what I generally see and what I want to hear. I create something that others find useful. I put my sharp knife in the service of others, if they need some cutting which they can't bring themselves to perform. I heal with knowledge, to the extent that I have it, with insight and poetry, voice and dance.

While I may pose metaphysical questions, what I'm always looking for is a useful application of the answers that I get. I always want to know who speaks, when my conscious mind speaks, and who speaks, when my unconscious mind speaks.

How do I listen when the conscious mind speaks? How do I listen when the unconscious mind speaks? How do I integrate the two, so I won't lose my balance?

The reason for this work is related to my sense of being in the world, and how useful and happy I can be in it. As a lover of non-dualism, I'm ecstatic all the time. I know exactly which button to push to conjure that perception of things and which enables me to see what a marvelous world this is. I also like it that we're all going to die. I'm never bored. I have the cards to thank for that.

Socially, while I take care of business, I prefer to focus my awareness on when it's appropriate to nail my latest diploma on the wall and when it's not. In other words, what I go for is this: How much time can I permit myself to spend in the muddy waters of the unconscious, where everything is allowed, and how much time can I allow myself to dominate the field for which I'm being paid to dominate? So time is crucial. If there's anything I resent the most – if I can ever use that word, as it doesn't fit my Zen Buddhist inclinations – then, it's wasting time. Giving Caesar what Caesar wants can be a major waste of time. Likewise, wailing in some emotional and potentially depressing state can be even worse. Indeed, then, it makes sense to ask myself regularly about how appropriately I embody my social and private functions.

The point I'm trying to make here is that living the magical life requires asking many questions, and then discovering that most of the answers we get pertain to consolidating our place in the world. The ultimate magic is in knowing our place, so that we can act from within it with the force of that impenetrable mystery, which is the mystery of the obvious.

Before I move on to saying something about how we can make an invocation that takes our magic with the cards to the oracular, sacred space, where we get to hear something about just how poetic life and all living is, I want to pose this question to the cards, a question that brings our awareness closer to the thing itself, the thing that will never insult our soul, but rather invite it to connect to what is on the other side of our fears.

What is the most obvious in magic?

The Empress, The Emperor, 10 of Swords

Indeed, the cards are miraculous again. With a pack of cards in my hands I am on a never ending journey of marvel. I hardly ever experience a situation when I don't make big eyes at the cards, as if seeing them for the first time. All the elements rush through me at once, dissociating too, attracting and repelling thoughts, contracting and expanding emotions. I see how the iron in my blood responds to the card of the 10 of swords, giving me a direct answer that's obvious, but which at the same time makes me want to keep asking more questions. That's also obvious.

The most obvious in magic is that the female and male forces are always at war. Working these forces in equal balance is deadly.

It's time to call the alchemists, once more.

SPELLCRAFT
BASIC PRINCIPLES

*The base of all forms of magic however or by whomever used must be
the same fundamentally, and that base is Mind.
Mind is the instrument, the channel and perhaps in some cases the
creator of the forces which produce 'magical' results.*

– Justine Glass, *Witchcraft: The Sixth Sense*

There are many theories about what a spell is, or what the
function of spellcraft is. Some of these theories make specific ref-
erences to written records, while others claim meaning in the
name of a tradition passed down to us the oral way[1].

For the sake of neutrality, let us make a reference to the dictionary – the very repository of words – and consider the etymology of the word 'spell' (from the Online Dictionary of Etymology):

---

1   See Robin Skelton's book, *Spellcraft* (1978) that addresses both the nature of
    spellcrafting, as it is anchored in the poetry of the oracular, and its oral
    transmission. For an older source that tackles the notion that the mind is
    primordial for a practitioner of magic, especially for the one who is not
    among the elect, and for whom spirits present themselves as a matter of
    course, see Cornelius Agrippa's *Three Books of Occult Philosophy* (1531-1533).

spell (n.1)

Old English *spell* "story, saying, tale, history, narrative, fable; discourse, command," from Proto-Germanic **spellam* (see **spell** (v.1)). Compare Old Saxon *spel*, Old Norse *spjall*, Old High German *spel*, Gothic *spill* "report, discourse, tale, fable, myth;" German *Beispiel* "example." From c. 1200 as "an utterance, something said, a statement, remark;" meaning "set of words with supposed magical or occult powers, incantation, charm" first recorded 1570s; hence any means or cause of enchantment.
The term 'spell' is generally used for magical procedures which cause harm, or force people to do something against their will – unlike charms for healing, protection, etc. ["Oxford Dictionary of English Folklore"]

If we use this as a starting premise for practical work, then let us declare out loud that what we shall be doing here, in following the guidelines for the basic principles in spellcraft, is work with the crafting of words into which we breathe a certain power, so that the words will end up performing something other than just plain communication (I write, you read).

We add intention to the communicative aspect of words, but unlike the type of intention that is there by default in all acts of communication – which enables us to understand each other – in spellcrafting this intention is aligned with an analogous visual image of what is desired manifest. That is to say, this intention is based on an act of, first, 'fetching' a visual image that is charged with the highest emotion from the pool of personal experience and, second, ordering it verbally to perform a specific and concrete task.

In this sense we make a crucial distinction between real power and symbolic power. As words are the symbolic manifestation of our general desire to communicate, in spellcrafting the idea is to go behind this symbolism and conjure a sense of a performative dance with words. By allowing the words to dance with us, we assign them a magical function.

How does this function manifest?

THOUGHT · FAITH · BREATH

There is a simple visual exercise that comes from my own practice, based on age-old common sense and universal ability to imagine a scene as it unfolds concomitantly with the viewing of a 'real' event as it passes before our eyes. For instance, as I'm writing these words down, I look at my computer screen, past the marginal vision of my bookshelf, which I also see clearly with the corner of my eye, and all the while allowing for the image of my memory of hiking to a sacred place on the Lofoten Islands in the Norwegian Arctic to unfold.

While writing these words, I can, at the same time, clearly conjure into my head not only the whole itinerary and the geography of the landscape in Norway, but also the smell of the place, the temperature, and the general, strong feeling of anticipating meeting the spirits of some dead folks from the Iron Age.

While writing these words down, and thinking about my theory here, I can also perfectly clearly conjure the question I had posed to myself at the time of my wandering through the wilderness, having to do with speculating about what form these spirits would take and whether I would get a sense of their presence at all; all this beyond noting the layout of the burial stones and other such cultural structures.

Now, if I were to perform a spell at this very moment, perhaps one of protection, or one of necromantic ability, I should be able to 'fetch' all these feelings I've had associated with my real walk in nature, and bring them closer to what I imagine I want manifest right now.

Once I do that, I can then start verbalizing an invocation, incantation, a curse, or an enchantment that draws on these two parallel experiences:

1) the experience of focalizing my desire into a familiar feeling, or thought of a strong emotional response to the world;

2) the experience of transposing the imagined unto the real, not symbolic power of the law of pretending.

The magical dictum: 'Fake it till you make it' is a good one, though in order for the experiencing of real power to take place, one would have to consider the extent to which the faking of it occurs on both planes of perception: the inner and the outer, the mental and the material. In magic, it's no good pretending that you like something and make that known to the world, while at the same time thinking silently to yourself that the thing you're trying very hard to like is actually horrible – and this you won't tell the world a word about.

In magic we seek the law of correspondence as it aligns with inner and outer forms of expressions. If I must pretend that I like something, then I must see myself acting towards the real manifestation of liking the thing, both as I show it to the world, and as I think it to myself. That's the art: To match the inner to the outer to perfection.

THINK IT · WANT IT · SAY IT

Let us attempt a first 'general rehearsal' exercise. Think of this exercise as the backbone of everything that you will be doing when performing magic. This is the beginning of spellcrafting, and the end, if you like. The perfect circle. But first, here are some general guidelines:

- You conjure a thing into being through the backdoor of your imagination.
- You feel the force of the imagined infuse your desire to make the thing you want manifest.
- You start talking. You participate in the creation of a 'story, saying, tale, history, narrative, fable, discourse, command'.
- You start seeing. Depending on the context, you can choose a token that will link you with a validation of the truthfulness of what you're doing.

All magical thinking works by analogy. The memory of one event together with all its emotional charge can be transposed onto something else in the present moment, something that is desired highly. If you venerate your own desire long enough, strongly enough, you will make your desire shine, take shape and function, become, or turn into what you want. One memory can muster enough energy to kill a horse, or heal a bird.

So the act of fetching a memory of a real event that you can see unfold right before your eyes – while you may also sit at the breakfast table stuffing yourself with cornflakes and wondering about the meaning of life – begins in the belief that you can do all this. You can be in two places at the same time. Even better: You can be beyond time. You can create a close relationship between your memory of an image, or event, with all that it entails, and the image of what you want to achieve.

One thing to remember is that although all magic begins in the mind, without proper grounding of the mental in the material there's no successfulness. It is for this reason that the shamans of old told their apprentices to visualize real places in nature, where they could start their flights to the otherworld. The idea is to 'see' it and then put your finger imprint on it. Know that only your real love and hatred, or such similar powers, can move your imaginary mountains. Power itself is never imaginary, even though the path we choose to direct this power through may well be.

ACT BECOMES (F)ACT

Try the following:

- Sit in a garden, or by a window, in your office where there are other people, or watch some art on TV.
- Select an element to focus on (a flower, the opposing balcony, your colleague's family portrait on her desk, the formal composition of a scene).
- Pick a strong memory of anything from the past (though love and hate are the strongest).
- Fetch it from its place and bring it close to what you're observing at hand.
- While you're observing whatever else, making random narratives about their place in the world, allow for this memory to unfold in as precise a manner as it was taking place at the time you experienced it.

- Hold these images together. See for yourself how easy it is to maintain two different points of focus, and their simultaneous unfolding.

- Transpose the memory image of all that you sense, smell, hear, see, and taste unto your activity in the present moment. Which of the 5 senses is the strongest? Is it the tactile sense? The feeling of a sharp knife through your heart? Dissolving in tears of pain or joy until you can't see anything anymore? Can you shred the family portrait on your colleague's desk to pieces? How much force do you feel when you do that? What words come out of your mouth as you engage in the act? Can you kiss the ground you stand on, in sheer gratitude for the perfect flower that the earth gives you as a gift? How beatific do you feel when you do that? What are the words of your song of praise? Can you feel the blessing of the earth? Can you pass it on to what you want to see manifest as happy? What words would you use here?

Basically this is the simplest and the most efficient recipe for magical spellcrafting: The holding together of two unrelated images (one present, one past) in order to create an emotion that brings about the future manifestation of what the conjoined imaginary timings show. And then saying it. Your words must follow your act. They must embody your desire, your enflamed heart. They must imitate the rising and falling tone of your acts, express the gravity of the situation, or the elevated emotions.

We have rhymes and cadences for all this. We have flow and interruptions. Say it all with your body. Let your body dictate the words. Bring your body constantly into your awareness that you have an intention. A strong intention. Your words, as they are written with your body, must give life to this intention. Use your breath to blow life into your intention, and let the words support your acts.

Magic is making gestures: bidding and beckoning, binding and blurring, blowing and blasting. (A)BRACADABRA...

Finally you can test your ability to do this in magical space. Select a token that links you to your act of intentionally bringing together two images in order to give magical life to a third reality. As we are not yet past this introduction, and as we are not yet making a spell for a specific scope, let us take a random token: You can decide that in the next three days you will spot a specific color in the public space, one of your own choice. It can be an ordinary color, or if you want to challenge your own magic, you can pick a color that's hard to find.

You can also do something else that you will recognize instantly as being your sign; something odd, or out of the ordinary. Take this gift of the color, or the odd occurrence, and thank it for validating your intentions and magic.

NOTE ON ETHICS

Before I move on to some final examples, I want to make clear once again my position, which is aligned with what I have already elaborated in the previous chapters. The technique I teach here is based entirely on my own understanding of what magic is, both at the experiential level and at thought level.

This techique deals with raw power and how we learn to use it. Power is power. Neither black nor white. While we don't question power, we can question the ways we use it or abuse it. In teaching it, however, I don't find it my place to instruct on how others should use power. Just as it's not for me to judge people's motivations for learning whatever craft, so it is not for me to evaluate how others elect to make use of what they learn.

All I can say is, may the force be with you!

INVOCATION

A lot has been written about spellcrafting, and about how we define a spell. If you have the time, I'd recommend reading the books of Jan Fries, Paul Huson, and Austin Osman Spare. There are others, but what I like about these three is that they all define spellcrafting as a way of sending a message to your deep mind, which is basically your unconscious. Why the deep mind? Because for a spell to work it must become part of the unconscious. If it doesn't, then it merely remains the reflection of the ego, and as we know, the ego always has an agenda that runs contrary to what the deepest, unconscious desires manifest. These desires are not always of the orderly kind. They are transgressive and powerful. Hence, the ego tries to regulate them. The ego's function is to censor everything, and make sure that your name is reputable. The ego is very big on your image, and how you project it into the world. But this regulation is not magic. It's culture. With magic, the first thing that we want to actually achieve is to move away from cultural pre-conditioning so that we may come closer to what is real, to what is not a dictation.

When we talk about the unconscious we talk about that part of our minds that we cannot access except through means that resemble trickery. It's not for nothing that we say, 'fake it till you make it'. The only way in which we can access our deep mind is if we trick our conscious mind about what we're doing. Hence the perception that what we're doing when doing magic is rather silly. But silliness is an important part of the process.

However, being systematically silly in order to attract power, or power spirit to work with – and here I mean it as a way of exchange rather than hierarchy – is like devotion, and that is the key to opening the gate to creating a spell that works. If you're devoted to what you're doing, no matter how silly it may look to yourself or from the outside perspective, then chances are that you will be conjuring just the power spirit that you need for your specific work.

Think of an invocation as an invitation, rather than even a conjuring, as this latter term has a history that implies orders and commands. From where I'm standing I'm not much for ordering spirits around. I would rather that they presented themselves to me, to my deep mind, or my imagination, as helpers, not as beings that are under my command.

But what is a spirit, and whom do we invoke into our sacred space when we do it? Let's check with the dictionary of etymology again. I like this one, as it gives us the history of the words.

spirit (n.)

mid-13c., "animating or vital principle in man and animals," from Anglo-French spirit, Old French *espirit* "spirit, soul" (12c., Modern French esprit) and directly from Latin *spiritus* "a breathing (respiration, and of the wind), breath; breath of a god," hence "inspiration; breath of life," hence "life;" also "disposition, character; high spirit, vigor, courage; pride, arrogance," related to *spirare* "to breathe," from PIE *(s)peis* – "to blow" (cognates: Old Church Slavonic pisto "to play on the flute").

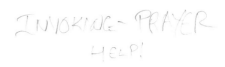

What I like in this list is the idea that spirit is related to breath. A breath that's animated. So when we invoke spirits into our space to help us with our magical task, we invite a second breath. This can take various shapes. Some perceive it as a burning bush – just think of the famous Biblical story of Moses and his invocations. Others see things, and yet others hear or smell things. But what we need to remember is that this 'thing' is still a breath. When we invoke, we use our breath to call on another breath. Isn't that beautiful? But invoking also has a history. It means to give voice to your breath. From Latin, *invocare,* to vocalize a call.

Let us now look at how we can all do it.

INVOCATION AND THE CARDS

To begin with, any act of invoking has to be tied to a clear intent. You are calling, but for what purpose? You will have to clear your intent before any act of invocation. Presently, as we don't know what each of you will want to seek, I will perform a divination with the cards to figure out what we could all, personally, focus on whenever we need to perform this ritual.

As a general ritual, the act of invoking is akin to a prayer. It simply means that you ask for help. This also means that you're willing to relinquish your own agency in terms of magical doings, and hand it over to whoever presents herself. You are asking for help with an issue. You get a sense of who is there listening to your petition. You formulate it, and then close. The closing means that you seal your breathing with faith. The listener will do your bidding because you have kindly asked for it, and because you trust that your request is granted. If your request is deemed questionable, you will also know it. The mirror on your table will fall off and break, or your candle will flicker in a way that's disturbing. Either way, you will know that you may need to revise your request, if that's the case. Acknowledge whatever comes, say thank you, and leave.

So here is a crucial question to the cards regarding how we can go about it more concretely (the example comes from a cycle of spellcrafting I have created for my student, Josie Close).

What will make my invocations powerful and efficient? What do I need to perform in addition to the standard calling: 'Here I am, I need this, who is here to help me out?'

The cards that fell on my table are beautiful and address precisely that which is quite universal for an invocation. They tell us that we don't need to deviate from received traditions. The message here is very clear and crisp.

The Magician, The Devil, The Pope

The Magician tells us that we need an altar. Create a space, quite literally have a table, which we can put a few things on that have significance for our purpose. We can use an item that represents our four elements: Fire, air, water, earth. We may also want to have at the center of our altar an object signifying what we're asking for. It's up to us what we deem appropriate. But we must always use our common sense, and remember that our object must bear a resemblance to what we're asking for. If it's love, we can use something red to represent it, as that resembles our blood running through our heart, pumping up the adrenaline. Our blood rushing.

The Devil is clearly telling us to have confidence in our calling. We can use our hand in our invocation. Extend our arm and have our palm flat, fingers slightly bent, as if to capture the spirit. I find this image very apt. The Devil also tells us that we must be prepared to accept any spirit that comes through, whether from the above or the below. We must not be afraid. We may face our own demons if we must, but we must be devoted to our act of calling.

We must also be prepared for several spirits to come through, and then make sure they understand who's in command. As we call, it's our turf. We must demand that our place is respected. If we feel something is not right, we can make a dismissive gesture with our hand. Ask that whatever disturbs us go behind us and leave. Remind the spirits also that we have not created a protective circle for a purpose, and that we called only on the ones who are willing to help, not the ones who disregard the act of hospitable courtesy.

When we're done, we must make sure that we close the ritual properly. Close the sacred space by extinguishing our candle, if we used one, or the smoke that still burns, if we used incense.

We can give a benediction, like the Pope. Bless ourselves to begin with, and then bless our sacred space. Bless also the spirits that came through. Say, thank you and amen, or some other word of power that indicates our desire for the things asked for to come to pass: 'So mote it be. This space is now closed.'

As we can see, so far the cards have completely supported what we also read about in the books that some folklorists have taken the pains to write. This is a good sign.

WITH THIS BREATH I TAKE THEE

But if we return for a while to the idea of making an invocation based on our breath inviting another breath to participate in our magic, then we can make a reference to the lore that emphasizes the idea of reciting poems.

All spiritual traditions distinguish between invocation and bidding, and we can often see how the calling gets mixed up with the request. Take these lines, for instance:

Oh great spider, come, oh, come,
Oh great spider, come,
Show me justice, oh, great spider
Show me justice done.

This is a verse I once made for myself, and which I repeated three times, as often is the case with all charms and enchantments. As you can see, I here follow the rule of calling, invoking a concrete power that I associate with the spider, and then I do the bidding, where I concretely ask the spider to render me justice.

In terms of the formal approach, I cannot stress it strongly enough: Keep it simple. Use simple words, and if you can create a rhyme, then you're set. Spirits like a good chanting voice too, a good melody and rhythm, or a strong musical command. It is not for nothing that we find rhymes populating all the traditional magical invocations that we now find in old grimoirs.

So here is when the exercise of visualizing yourself in two places at the same time becomes crucial. On the one hand, you sit in your sacred space – this can be within a circle that you cast, if that's your preference, or simply standing by an altar – and on the other hand, you see yourself standing in a place analogical to where you want to see your magic performed. If it's the magic courthouse you need to conjure, then create that space accordingly. Make it stern and rigid and cold. The law is the law, and it knows no mercy. Truth is not about mercy. The spider is a good ally to have if you need to tread the web of justice.

ACTION

Open ritual space.
Make an invocation.
Use a simple rhyming spell.
Close ritual space.

Write down your experience.

- What time of day did you perform it?

- How long did it take until you sensed a presence? It's a good idea to take your time, actually. After your invocation wait a few minutes to sense the atmosphere in the room, if you're in a house. You may want to do this while the window is open. Think of the invocation as an invitation to a party. Do you have anything on your altar to offer the spirits? Have some libation, food, and the like, all according to whom you'd like to come. If it's no one in particular you have in mind, but you make an invocation for anyone to come who can help you with your issue, then keep it simple. A mix of water and bread is enough. Or milk and honey.

- If you have concrete sensations of something happening in the room, what can you report happened when you stated your request? Did you get an answer? How concrete was the impression of what you need to do?

- Upon closing the ritual, what feeling about your own performance did you have? Did you feel like the Pope? If you didn't, revise your attitude, and ask yourself, why not, what did I forget?

REFLECTION

One of the things that I'm attracted to whenever I read poetry is the realization that the skillful poet manages to put across his voice and his breath without flogging to death the topic that he writes about, or the muse that he invokes.

A good invocation must have something of the same quality. Above all, we must remember not to try too hard and thus ruin our experience with our eagerness. Whatever we must say, we must say it with dreamy eyes, squinting and allowing for shapes to take form.

What an invocation does is to create space between the others and us. The art is in knowing how and where to keep our distance so that magic can unfold before our eyes while the spirits are singing and clapping, and teaching us what there is to know, the poetry of the essential journey, intoning perhaps to Emily Dickinson's song of the soul:

I have an errand imminent
To an adjoining Zone.

VERBARIUM

We are reaching the end of this journey. I could write more on some other forms of spellcraft, but the truth is that I believe that if we can make a successful invocation then we will also be able to perform the other forms of classical spells in this repertoire associated with incantation, blessing, protection, healing, love, binding, and bidding. The only thing that may change in these, and would be different from the type of invocation I have described above, is the wording and the tone of how we formulate what we want.

For instance, I have an enchantment against the evil eye that I always recite in Romanian, as it blends a quick command in tone with the performative action of having words literally chase away the ailment so that the wind gets so mad as to dissipate the hell out of it. There is a doubling of action here insofar as the words that come out of the mouth literally spell out what the mouth has done, using the breath to push the words out of it and the wind as a receiver: 'With my own mouth I'm saying that you're gone to the mad wind...' The evil that was cast also has a mouth, but this mouth is now reached by the wind invoked, and messed up by the breath of the sorcerer. It's a beautiful spell and I wish I could offer a translation, but that would ruin what is going on at the level of the sound, performing several actions at the same time.

But it goes to show that the only condition necessary for the successful performance of spells is that one understands exactly the context of what needs to be done and why, so that one acquires the necessary gravity of tone, or lightness of the phrase that needs to go into it. A good spell is truly a work of art from a poetic point of view, and the sophistication that some display can be astonishing. Any anthology of spells that folklorists in nearly every country have put together will give you an idea.

Some would say that props and costumes are also necessary. Indeed the theatricality of standing by an altar fully adorned in silk, masks, and protective stones and salts is not to underestimate, but I believe that what ultimately does it is the prayer, the words that come from the right place and are intoned at just the right resonance so that the whole body vibrates in unison with the evoked emotion. That's the art: To say it like it is, yet keep the mystery.

We can keep the mystery by allowing our minds to enter a state of beatitude, by enchanting ourselves over what needs to be done. This is the form an incantation takes. An incantation operates with a repetitive cadence, and is often a first person invocation that can run like this, in my own words:

I am come today, I am come.
I am come to see and sing.
I am come.

I am come to see the omen.
I am come to see the sign.
Come sign, come omen. Come.
I am come.
I'm the sign, the omen.
I am come.

Says Robin Skelton in his book, *Spellcraft:*

> The object of incantation is to put the conscious critical intelligence to sleep so that the intuitive element can have full play, and so that the 'message' may be transmitted without qualifications by the conscious mind. (Skelton, 1998: 45)

In my own cartomantic practice, whenever I want to heighten the poetic style I begin with an incantation. I have found that incantations are particularly useful in readings for third parties. As people's curiosity has no bounds, I get a lot of questions from folks who simply want to know what other folks are up to. Call it spying with the cards. As I have stated earlier, while I always use my critical sense, I do not position myself judgmentally vis-à-vis people's concerns. If they want to know about others, and trust what the cards suggest, so be it. From a storytelling point of view, curiosity never kills these cats, and what comes out of a reading for third parties can be both illuminating and entertaining.

In this context then, I have found that an incantation can have a function similar to what others call remote viewing (Mickaharic, 1995), which is to say, the ability to send forth your 'fetch', 'familiar' or astral body, if you prefer, to a distant place where you can view the unfolding of some event, or just survey the land.

While remote viewing requires advanced concentration techniques, through the use of incantation one can propel oneself straight into the imagery of the cards so that a sharper mode of seeing is enhanced, the kind of seeing that goes beyond accounting for the standard observations of the semantic composition of the elements in the cards.

To give an example: A man from Scotland wanted to know how his estranged friend in Denmark was doing, and he expressed the concern that his friend may have gone too conservative in his views after having married, what he called, 'the prototype of the Danish woman, project manager *extraordinaire,* for whom everything is a project, including the husband, the children, the job, the parents, the house, and the dog.' Yack. The idea was to get an insight into this household. While listening to more uncomfortable notions about the dangers of a life based on status quo ideals, I could hear forming into my head a small incantation, something that involved a cock and a hen, a raven and a dove. I laid down three cards, and, 'the horror, the horror.'

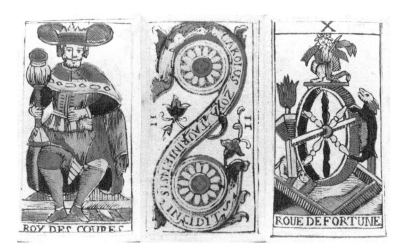

The man of the house, the King of Cups, did turn contractual, and what we can suggest was viewed at the remote level was a ribbon inscribed for all to see with the names of all in the house. We both started laughing at what we imagined was a long line of names on the door and the mailbox, which we didn't see in the cards, but could see forming right before our eyes, perhaps saying indeed: Here lives a family project, all stamped in the right places and going somewhere. But where exactly?

What we saw next, and which ultimately confirmed the Scot's suspicion was a Wheel of Fortune that somehow didn't give the impression of good fortune at the level that matters. Dehumanized creatures are pinned to it, going up and down with the routine and the predictable program. Good project on the outside, heralding a respectable name, but on the inside, lord have mercy: The very definition of status quo. Now, it is very likely that we could have arrived at this same conclusion without the incantation, but I can safely say that the cock and the hen, the raven and the dove, lent a particular voice to the visual message, and had the flavor of the oracular, not only confirming the suspicion but also performing it. Not long after this the Scot heard from his friend. He thought that he sounded boring in his expressing of righteous opinions about family values, and that he used the worst cliché phraseology to describe his domestic bliss. Indeed, we could ask Freud what he would make of this demonstrative act of enunciation that discloses the poverty in inauthentic living: If you have to say that you *are* (happy, rich, content, powerful), you *aren't*. On the other hand, as The King of Cups enjoys the wheeling bond, any judgment against it would be an act of futility.

The point about an incantation is that it allows us to appreciate an entry point to neutrality. As it is fantasy that rules the mythopoetic act, our magic gets strengthened by the flow of speaking creatures, instructing us in the art of graceful deliverance.

BLESSING, BINDING, BIDDING

Whereas a blessing is an utterance of protection, and often takes the form of the direct second person address: 'You be blessed', the binding and the bidding are acts of control, often using the form of invocation, 'You come,' addressed to the natural forces such as the wind, or fire, a demon, or a spirit, 'and do such and such to this other person'. The same amount of energy must be pushed forward as in an invocation, and the same repetitive incantatory words can be used to convey the final message: 'It is done'. The phrases, 'So mote it be,' or 'If it be the Lord's will', emphasize a sealing of the binding words as a form of bidding. Or at least that's my understanding of what underlies the basic principles here.

The primary purpose of a binding spell is to stop someone in their tracks; basically to prevent them from behaving in whatever way they behave that is not aligned with the wishes of the binder.

For instance, if you want to make a girl fall in love with you, but you can see that she's ignoring you, you can then create a spell that would stop her from ignoring you. If your colleague at work feels entitled to get ahead of you, you can spell out a binding of him to his chair and thus render him impotent in the run for promotions. If someone tramples on your head in disrespect, you can trample on theirs, by enchanting a piece of paper with their names on it that you then put into your shoes. Every time you take a step, you step on their heads. You do this with enough conviction and strength of character – though make sure to distinguish between mere stubbornness and real strength – and you will see how quickly their popularity will decline.

A binding spell can also be used to tie the magician to a location. For instance, shamans of old would never travel to the underworld without an enchanted magic cord tied to their bodies. A nine feet long strand of red wool or silk is a classic, and has the function of connecting the magician to a protected and familiar space. For the creation of such a cord, all one needs is power words whispered into its knotting. The cord is long enough to allow for the incantation to take over your consciousness and shift it into magical mode. By the time you're done you will discover that you will be magically and quite perfectly insane.

These are all folk magic remedies found in every culture. What they have in common is the idea of sympathetic magic that follows the law of similitude and symmetry. We are here with the Old Testament, dictating, 'an eye for an eye', not with the preaching about turning the other cheek for more slapping.

Some find all binding spells questionable from an ethical point of view, but we are not here to judge. Oftentimes the ones who raise objections have some skeletons in their closet too, disclosing just how much ego of their own they have enthroned when they try to usurp that of others. But a good magician is not into proving who is to be master. The very sign of a good magician is in her ability to be above dogma, verification and consensus reality.[2]

A good magician works with power not hierarchy, and she knows how to discern between what is essential and what is not. A good magician will also apply her basic knowledge of right and wrong to a magical working that situates itself above dualism. And that is the ultimate art: To know that when power moves through you, it shifts your consciousness. The catch is to become one with this power so much so that you stop judging against it.

───────

2   See also Carolyn Elliott's apt essay: '7 Insane Keys to Practical Magic' (2015).

TAKE TWO

How can we use the cards for a binding situation? In two ways: First as a divinatory tool, measuring, on the one hand, the pulse of the spell – is this spell strong enough? – and on the other hand, assessing the form its necessity must take – paper or puppet? Second, we can use the cards as sympathetic objects.

Once my sister decided to join me on my annual vacation in Norway. I was already on top of a mountain when she had decided to drive up to the cabin – a rather long way from Copenhagen. As this was her first drive through another country, I was anxious for her. I asked the cards about the situation.

The Charioteer and the Tower didn't look too good together in a string of three cards, with the disaster card in the last position. I said to her: 'You're going to have an accident.' I then immediately proposed that she did some magic.

'Take the card of Temperance from the pack,' I said, 'enchant it with words of power for protection on the road and balanced driving, and you'll be set. If we can't prevent the accident, we can at least hope for a mild consequence.' I then waited and waited for her to show up, way past the estimated time for her arrival. I knew it. She had an accident. My head went down in a contemplative mode, as I felt a twinge of dissapointment. Why didn't the spell work? Finally she called me: 'I had an accident. Some idiot bumped into me, nothing major, but we had to wait for the police and it just dragged and dragged.' 'Oh, hell, at least Temperance kept it in check,' I said, while secretely wishing that her spell had been stronger.'

Then my sister dislosed something in a sheepish way: 'You know, I never did what you said. I didn't take any enchanted card on board with me. Sorry.' 'What?', I blurted at her in exasperation. I told her that next time she was going to disregard the possibility of protection, it would be her funeral.

This was an example of bidding whose function was to perform a protection. A simple and efficient one, yet missed. But the thought of it counted enough. My sister arrived unharmed.

POWER WORDS

The thing to consider in spellcrafting is that we are never concerned with what value we ascribe to words. Spellcrafting words are not just words. They are words of power. And as I said before, power is power, neither good nor bad. Consequently, in spellcrafting it is quite pointless, and not to mention running counter to the very function of power words, to decide beforehand that a spell is positive or negative. A spell is a spell. A burst of power. If something needs binding, we will use the words that would describe that very act. The act itself has no inherent value. If something needs breaking, vanquishing, or banishing, then we will use the very words that perform these acts.

In spellcrafting it will not do to assign positive value to an act whose motives are questionable because we may feel bad about our morals. If you want to bind your adrenaline driven colleague to his chair, you will not craft your words of power by invoking the good God: 'Dear God, I'm a good person, but I would really like this selfish bastard to stop trampling on my head.' No, you will find words that will match your desire to do away with the useless competition to perfection.

Many are disturbed by enchantments, black magic, or sorcery that makes recourse to words of power that can hurl a brick at someone and stop them in their tracks. They will do anything to put an end to the woman who can single-handedly redirect the orientation of the wind, using simple words of power. In its more benign manifestation, the rejection of wizards will translate into a form of dismissal: 'It's all superstition'.

But the real reason why spellcrafting disturbs is because it uses language at its most performative and undifferentiating function. Cultural critics have long been pointing to the damaging aspect of language and its discursive power[3]. Indeed, what has worked for imperialists is true of what works for magicians. From a cultural standpoint, language which manipulates and controls is negative. From a magical point of view, this same language is positive, insofar as it gets things done. It is up to the magician herself how she chooses to approach power, whether it be used for her blessings or curses.

---

3   See the work of Michel Foucault, particularly *Power* (The Essential Works of Foucault, 1954-1984, Vol. 3), 2001. The New Press.

IN THE NAME OF LOVE

Love spells are countless and can take many forms. But I like to think of what is going on when we engage in creating a love spell. We say that when we're in love we can feel the blood rushing through our veins like there is no tomorrow. Why not, then, use blood itself to accompany our heightened emotion and our poetic verbal punch? 'Oh, Romeo, wherefore art thou Romeo?' Shakespeare immortally invoked eternal love, when he allowed Juliet to let the spirit of love move through her. Neither Juliet nor Romeo made any blood offerings – they took poison – but I wonder what kind of love story would have emerged had they done that.

Formally, a love spell uses the same invocatory and incantatory breath as all the other spells, whether they be of a blessing, binding, bidding, or breaking character. The power words used to evoke the desired emotion must be of the same performative nature as in the other spells. The only catch is that in order for the spell to work, the magician must be detached from the object of desire, and that is a tall order when love is at stake. Nothing is more possessive than love. Perhaps it is for this reason that many seek the service of a fortuneteller or a magician when they need this working done. A wise decision. Alternatively, spill a few drops of your own blood on your words written on parchment. Let the skin absorb the iron. Sit back and watch the power of attraction unfold your way. Rose petals, red candles, and other love related paraphernalia that takes care of creating a sympathetic setting can also help, but the best are still the words themselves and the power you use to push them forward. Breathe in the coolness of your head and breathe out the heated passion of your gut.

Here is an example of two love spells that use not only the classical way of composing a magical and rhythmical cadence, with words performing the deed, but also the cards against whose backdrop the spells have been composed.

For these spells I have used a plain playing-card deck. The first spell follows the imagery of the Queen of Hearts, 5 of Hearts, and 8 of Spades. The second spell follows the imagery of the Ace of Diamonds, 2 of Spades, 7 of Hearts and Ace of Clubs. I have let these cards dictate the intensity of the emotion, as you can see in the poems that came out of it.

For the first spell I have used a flying ointment based on mandrake root. I simply anointed myself with it, spreading it evenly in thick layers over my temples, my wrists, and my heart.

For the second spell I have used a blood offering. You can guess which one gave me the strongest response: The blood spell. It simply made my hair rise, and I kept marveling in stupor for a while at my own words. I can still swear that I have no idea where those words came from. I find moments like these to be highly poetical, and indicative of what any spellcrafter wants to achieve in the end, a sense of union with the time when all words were power words, the time when words were all magical, the time when clichés did not exist, the time when power roamed freely through us, and stirring major magical shifts in our consciousness and holy imagination.

At the time I did these spells some of the emotion and desire that went into them spilled on parchment in the form of ink, oil, and blood, giving voice to talismanic drawings. Sometimes what comes out of it is a sigil in the tradition of the Picatrix, but at other times my drawings simply just work with the bones and stones on my table, root and wild flowers, or some other magical prompters.

The Queen's root is divided into five hearts.
The sign of the body.
Five spots are anointed and the sixth gets an extra push by
the indexical finger dipped in mandrake.
Opening the heart needs help.
The imagination turns black on the eighth count
leaving room for all on call to state their names.
Chronophagoi.
Ally on ally – All-y, All-y
Al-kal-o-id is the mantra of the time eaters.
A purple breath is behind the Queen's back.
Her earrings absorb the sense-u-al unknown.
All rise for the lawless covenant.
The naked and the cloaked play a game of poison.

Love in symmetry is a mysterious dance.
A dance of stars.
The crossing hearts are marking the spot,
fetching the X.
The coup de grâce on behalf of the cross blows the breath
saying:
Let there be light and love and a strong body.

The spell be impaled.

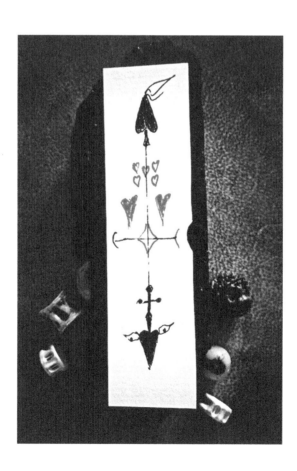

The primary motor in the crafting of spells is to let your magical mood be enhanced by the cards to the point where you can hear your words take hold of you, seize your heart, and your ordinary consciousness. The idea is to get to a point of insanity where you could swear that you can hear your own words being swirled about, and frightening the hell out of you.

The use of cards for all spells and magical work can follow either the divinatory function, where it will be your interpretative skills that will drive forward the poetic narrative force in your crafting, or the intervening function, where you allow your words to choose you, to dance you beyond your cognitive capacity into the space that's greater than what you think, and how you judge yourself against your own desires.

I have asked the cards to provide me with a final word, as there can be no final conclusion to a life based on magical training and practice.

The Magician, The Popesse, and the Star have sent me to the beginning of this last chapter where I laid down three principles of magical thinking. Indeed, think it, have faith, and breathe it.

REFERENCES

Agrippa, Henry Cornelius (2006). *Three Books of Occult Philosophy.* Trans. James Freake. Llewellyn's Publications.

Caldwell, Ross S., Depaulis, Thierry, Ponzi, Marco (2010). *Explaining the Tarot: Two Italian Renaissance Essays on the Meaning of the Tarot Pack.* Maproom Publications.

Calvino, Italo (1979). *The Castle of Crossed Destinies.* Mariner Books.

Camoin, Philippe and Jodorowsky, Alejandro (1997-ongoing). International Tarot School. [https://en.camoin.com/] Last accessed: December 12, 2014.

Candrea, I.A. (1944). *Folklorul medical român comparat. Privire generala. Medicina magica.* Bucuresti.

Depaulis, Thierry (2005). 'Cartes et cartiers dans les anciens états de Savoie (1400-1860).' In *Journal of the International Playing-Card Society.* Nr. 4, April 2005.

——— (2013). 'The Tarot de Marseille: Facts and Fallacies.' In *The Journal of the International Playing-Card Society.* Vol. 42, No. 1 and No.2, July-December 2013.

Darche, Claude (1994). *La Pratique du tarot de Marseille: Spiritualité et Divination.* Les Editions du Rocher.

Davies, Owen (2009). *Grimoires. A History of Magic Books.* Oxford University Press.

David, Jean-Michel (2009). *Reading the Marseille Tarot.* Association for Tarot Studies Publishing.

Decker, Ronald, Depaulis, Thierry, Dummett, Michael, (1996). *A Wicked Pack of Cards: The Origins of the Occult Tarot.* St. Martin's Press.

DuQuette, Lon Milo (2010). *Low Magic.* Llewellyn Publications.

Elias, Camelia (2015). *Marseille Tarot: Towards the Art of Reading.* EyeCorner Press.

———— (2015). '3 Ways of Reading Cards Like the Devil'. In *Bad Witches: Magic for Smart People.* [http://badwitch.es/]

———— (2014). 'The Arts of the Night: Circumventing the Sign.' In *The Magiculum.* Ed. Todd Landman. EyeCorner Press.

———— (2012). 'HE RECO ME: Enrique Enriquez's Poetics of Divination: Introduction'. In *En Terex It. Encounters around the Tarot* by Enrique Enriquez. EyeCorner Press.

———— (2010). *Taroflexions.* Cartomancy and Magic Blog. [https://taroflexions.wordpress.com/]

———— (2015). *Cartomancy.* A bi-monthly column. Agora Patheos. [http://www.patheos.com/blogs/agora/category/columns/cartomancy/

———— (2015). 'Suggesting Living'. In *The Cartomancer: A Quarterly Tarot, Lenormand & Oracle Journal.* Vol. 1, Issue 1. Summer 2015.

———— (2015). 'No Magic, and Ishtar's Song.' Essay and Prose Poem. In *Return to Mago.* [http://magoism.net/2015/07/06/essay-and-prose-poem-no-magic-and-ishtars-song-by-camelia-elias/]

Eliade, Mircea (1964). *Shamanism: Archaic Techniques of Ecstasy.* Princeton University Press.

Elliott, Carolyn (2015). '7 Insane Keys to Practical Magic'. *In Bad Witches: Magic for Smart People.* [http://badwitch.es/7-insane-keys-to-practical-magic/]

Enriquez, Enrique (2011). *Tarology.* EyeCorner Press.

———— (2012). *En Terex It: Encounters around the Tarot.* Vol. 1. EyeCorner Press.

———— (2012). *Ex Itent Er: Encounters around the Tarot.* Vol. 2. EyeCorner Press.

Farley, Helen (2009). *A Cultural History of Tarot: From Entertainment to Esotericism.* I B Tauris & Co Ltd.

Flornoy, Jean-Claude (2007). *Le pèlerinage des bateleurs.* Editions letarot.com.

Foucault, Michel (2001). *Power* (The Essential Works of Foucault, 1954-1984, Vol. 3). The New Press.

Frawley, John (2001). *The Real Astrology.* Apprentice Books.

———— (2002). *The Real Astrology Applied.* Apprentice Books.

Fries, Jan (1992). *Visual Magick: A Manual of Freestyle Shamanism.* Mandrake of Oxford.

Ginzburg, Carlo (1991). *Ecstasies. Deciphering the Witches' Sabbath.* Trans. Raymond Rosenthal. Chigaco University Press.

Glass, Justine (1978). Witchcraft: The Sixth Sense. Wilshire Book Company.

Gorovei, Artur (1990) 'Descântecele românilor'. In *Folclor si folcloristica.* Chisinau: Editura Hyperion.

Greenwood, Susan (2000). *Magic, Witchcraft, and the Otherworld.* Oxford: Berg.

———— (2005). *The Nature of Magic: An Anthropology of Consciousness.* Oxford: Berg.

———— (2009). *The Anthropology of Magic.* Oxford: Berg.

Greer, John Michael and Warnock, Christopher, trans. (2010). *The Picatrix.* Adocentyn Press.

Guénon, René (2004). *Symbols of Sacred Science.* Sophia Perennis.

Jackson, Dawn R. (2006). *The Wise and Subtle Arte of Reading Cards as examined by a Witch who practices said Arte* [http://www.hedgewytchery.com/] Defunct website.

Huson, Paul (2004). *Mystical Origins of the Tarot: From Ancient Roots to Modern Usage.* Destiny Books.

Jodorowsky, Alejandro (2004). *The Way of Tarot.* Destiny Books.

Levi, Eliphas (1968). *Transcendental Magic: Its Doctrine and Ritual.* Trans. A. E. Waite. Weiser Books.

———— (2001). *The Key to the Great Mysteries.* Red Wheel/Weiser.

Marrone, Steven P. (2015). *A History of Science, Magic and Belief: From Medieval to Early Modern Europe.* Palgrave Macmillan.

Marteau, Paul (1949). *Le Tarot de Marseille.* Arts et Metiers Graphiques.

Mickaharic, Draja (1985). *Spiritual Cleansing: Handbook of Psychic Protection.* Weiser Books.

———— (1995). *Practice of Magic.* Weiser Books.

Miller, Jason (2009). *The Sorcerer's Secrets: Strategies in Practical Magick.* New Page Books.

Nicoara, Pavel (1961). *Despre preziceri, oracole si ghicit.* Editura Militara.

Olteanu, Antoaneta (1999). *Scoala de solomonie. Divinatie si vrajitorie in context comparat.* Bucuresti: Editura Paideia.

Papus (2008). *The Divinatory Tarot.* Aeon Books.

Parisse, Florian (2010) *Tarot de Marseille: Guide d'interprétation des 462 binômes.* Editions Trajectoire.

Ryan, Michael A. (2011) *A Kingdom of Stargazers: Astrology and Authority in the Late Medieval Crown of Aragon.* Cornell University Press.

Stanceanu-Putna, Andreiu Petru (1920). *Soarta omului sau viitorul descoperit prin carti.* Editura Cultura Romaneasca.

Semetsky, Ina (2011). *Re-symbolization of the Self: Human Development and Tarot Hermeneutic.* Sense Publishers.

Silvestre, Colette (1987). *Les Tarots.* Editions Grancher.

Skelton, Robin (1998) *Spellcraft.* Phoenix Publishing Inc.

Spare, Osman Austin (2001). *Ethos: Micrologus. The Books of Pleasure. The Witches Sabbath. Mind to Mind and How.* I-H-O Books.

Unger, Tchalaï (1985). *El Tarot.* Editiones Obelisco.

Vailente, Doreen (2007) *Natural Magic.* London: Robert Hale.

Von Franz, Marie-Louise (1986). *Number and Time: Reflections Leading Toward a Unification of Depth Psychology and Physics.* Northwestern University Press.

———— (2000). *Aurora Consurgens: A Document Attributed to Thomas Aquinas on the Problem of Opposites in Alchemy : A Companion Work to C.G. Jung's Mysterium Conjunctionis.* Von Franz, ed. Trans. R. F. C. Hull, A. S. B. Glover. Inner City Books.

———— (2001). *Psyche and Matter.* Shambhala.

Wilby, Emma (2006) *Cunning-Folk and Familiar Spirits: Shamanistic Visionary Traditions in Early Modern British Witchcraft and Magic.* Sussex Academic Press.

Williams, Paul (2008). 'The Poetry of the Tarot de Marseille.' At *Tarot Authentique.* [http://www.tarot-authentique.com/] Last accessed: December 12, 2014.

Znamensky, Andrei A. (2007). *The Beauty of the Primitive: Shamanism and Western Imagination.* Oxford University Press.

Lightning Source UK Ltd.
Milton Keynes UK
UKOW07f0522130815

256876UK00009B/33/P

9 788792 633286